CLAY PIGEON MARKSMANSHIP

CLAY PIGEON MARKSMANSHIP

By

PERCY STANBURY and G. L. CARLISLE

Photography by G. L. Carlisle

BARRIE & JENKINS
London Melbourne Sydney Auckland Johannesburg

Barrie & Jenkins Ltd

An imprint of the Hutchinson Publishing Group

17-21 Conway Street, London W1P 6JD

Hutchinson Publishing Group (Australia) Pty Ltd
PO Box 496, 16-22 Church Street, Hawthorne, Melbourne,
Victoria 3122

Hutchinson Group (NZ) Ltd
32-34 View Road, PO Box 40-086, Glenfield, Auckland 10

Hutchinson Group (SA) (Pty) Ltd
PO Box 337, Bergvlei 2012, South Africa

First published by Herbert Jenkins Ltd 1964
Reprinted 1968
Second edition 1971
Third edition 1974
Reprinted 1978, 1982 (with some updating), 1984
© Percy Stanbury and G. L. Carlisle 1964, 1974

Printed and bound in Great Britain by
Anchor Brendon Ltd, Tiptree, Essex

ISBN 0 214 20070 1

FOREWORD

by

LORD RUPERT NEVILL

Ex-President of the Clay Pigeon Shooting Association

I HAVE known Percy Stanbury for a very long time and have greatly admired not only his skill as a shot, but also his remarkable ability as an instructor with a profound knowledge of his subject. He is renowned as a coach of outstanding merit.

I therefore felt extremely delighted when I was asked to write a brief foreword to this book, which I have read with enthusiasm and pleasure. I am sure it will prove a most valuable manual for the beginner, as well as containing much that will interest and aid the marksman of ability.

The photographs by G. L. Carlisle are superbly presented, and this achievement of the two collaborators makes me feel that it will appeal not only to the initiates and dedicated ones for whom it was originally intended, but will succeed in arousing the enthusiasm of many other people.

Uckfield House,
Uckfield,
Sussex.

[5]

AUTHORS' PREFACE

1. This book describes the equipment needed by a clay pigeon shooter and how he should use it to get the best results. It tells the reader how to shoot straight.

2. The popularity of clay pigeon shooting is increasing, as is shown by the continual formation of new gun clubs and the growing number of entries in competitions. This is partly due to the new affluence enabling more people to buy guns while the opportunities of acquiring shooting rights become scarcer and more expensive.

3. Where 'dry' practice appears in the text it means going through the motions of shooting, handling a gun but not actually firing it.

4. References are made to 'normal' shooting, by which is meant the shooting of live creatures for sport and to eat, or because they are predators. Normal shooting, however, has different meanings according to localities and also to an individual's situation in life. The following definitions may help the uninitiated :

(a) In England, game shooting nearly always refers to driven birds, (mainly pheasants, partridges and grouse), although sometimes these are walked-up. It is expensive, the birds need to be looked after and are often artificially reared. Beaters are required to drive them.

(b) Walking-up is often regarded as an inferior form of game shooting usually associated with rough shooting, when a few friends search for the birds, preferably with the help of dogs. Most of the shots are inevitably taken at birds flying away from the guns, and they are easier than those at driven birds. Shooting grouse or partridges over pointers or setters, however, can be a most rewarding form of walking-up as regards the quality of the sport.

(c) Wildfowling means the shooting of geese, duck and waders along the shore and often out on the mud-flats exposed by the receding tide.

For more information on normal shooting readers are referred to "Shotgun Marksmanship" by the same authors.

5. The authors wish to express their thanks to those kind friends who allowed themselves to be photographed to demonstrate faults and good shooting style. Their thanks are also due to the Secretary of the Clay Pigeon Shooting Association for much helpful co-operation.

CONTENTS

LIST OF ILLUSTRATIONS

[11]

ILLUSTRATIONS

CLAY PIGEON MARKSMANSHIP

CHAPTER ONE

WHAT IS CLAY PIGEON SHOOTING?

CLAY pigeon shooting is a sport, a skill, perhaps even an art. Like any specialised pastime it embodies a certain use of language which may mystify the outsider in a manner surprising to its devotees. The ' clay ' target, for instance, is a saucer-shaped disc, about 4½ inches in diameter, not unlike an ashtray, and it is made of limestone and pitch; it is normally black but is sometimes of a different colour to make it more easily visible under certain conditions.

At the end of the 18th century live pigeons, released by hand, were sometimes used to practise the new sport of shooting birds on the wing and also to settle wagers on the skill of the participants. By the middle of the 19th century rules were formed to control pigeon shooting competitions and the birds were released from boxes known as ' traps ', and this word is still used, although now a trap is a device for throwing a clay pigeon. The early mechanical traps were simply metal springs which could be pulled down and released so that they flipped up and threw the target into the air; sometimes the target was a glass ball, perhaps filled with feathers. Trap shooting is mentioned in *The Sporting Magazine* in 1793 and American records show it to have become popular there by 1831, using the Hurlingham Club rules. The sport flourished and sparrows were occasionally used as the target; after 1880, when the first trap for throwing clays was made, development in the U.S.A. of mechanical traps was rapid.

When live pigeon shooting was made illegal in Great Britain in 1921 the mechanical trap improved here; the modern type is normally fixed in position, has a shot-proof housing built round it and can be adjusted to throw in many directions. The trap can also be released by remote control from behind the shooter.

When England accepted from America, in 1923, the automatic trap which could throw a series of clays at different angles selected at random, competitive shooting here assumed a more serious aspect. The usual procedure was for five shooters to position themselves in line about three yards apart and sixteen yards from the trap, and each shot in turn at single clays, calling for his target when he was ready, using the word 'Pull!' In the trap housing the 'trapper' loaded the trap and behind the shooters the 'puller' operated a lever connected by a rod, enclosed in a tube along the ground, to the trigger of the trap. When each of the shooters had had his turn they moved one position along to the right, No. 5 going round to No. 1's place, and the process was repeated. This was the start of what is now called 'Down-The-Line' shooting, or 'Trap Shooting', and it was not popular with some of the old live pigeon shooters; at one of the early meetings three of these old stagers had a go, found the shooting was not as easy as it had appeared ('just a simple going-away shot, you can't miss!') and decided that to follow the new sport would wear out their guns and use up too many cartridges. So they tipped their bowler hats to the company and departed.

Live pigeon shooting continued on the Continent, chiefly patronised by professionals who made good money going from place to place. At home, clay shooting soon gained in popularity, retaining the old cries whereby the target was still called a 'bird' and a hit was termed a 'kill', while a miss was referred to as 'lost'. In 1928 the Clay Pigeon Shooting Association was formed as a governing body, and most local clubs throughout the country became affiliated to it. The C.P.S.A. co-ordinates the dates of all the main shoots and it advises clubs on management, equipment, shoot lay-outs etc.; the Association organises the National Championships and also selects the teams for International matches. The weekly paper *Shooting Times and Country Magazine* is the official organ of the C.P.S.A. and it announces future fixtures and reports results of the more important competitions.

The shooting of clays may be undertaken for various reasons, as :

1. For initial instruction to the novice in the use of a shot-gun. This is best done at a Shooting School, although a trap or hand flinger may be set up on private ground with a 300 yard danger zone which can be kept clear of man and beast.

2. With instruction, to improve the experienced game shot's performance, with targets as nearly as possible simulating natural birds.

3. As a competitive sport, or, one might almost say, a game because there is a similarity to golf, for instance, in the need for skill, fitness, concentration and practice, and the object of achieving success in a minimum of strokes, or shots.

This book deals primarily with the competitive side of the clay game and, as with golf, the first thing for the new-comer to do is to join a club. There you will find a welcome and plenty of enthusiasts who will do their best to help you, to show you how to shoot and to demonstrate their varied equipment. You should not be disappointed at initial failures because in order to obtain good scores at clay shooting experience is necessary, and even a good shot cannot expect much success until he has learnt the tricks of the trade.

The clay target differs from the natural one in that, after very fast initial acceleration, it slows down and its flight path dips as it falls towards the ground. The good shot kills his bird very quickly, fifteen or twenty yards from the trap, but the inexperienced shooter will not even have his gun on the line of his target until it starts to fall, by which time he has a more difficult shooting problem to contend with, and the small size of the clay may allow it to escape unscathed through the shot pattern at the longer range. The speed of an expert trap shooter is indeed remarkable and to the inexperienced eye, almost magical: you will see him standing ready to shoot, alert and concentrating. He calls 'Pull!', his gun fires and as you hear the report and possibly even before you have seen the clay leave the traphouse, you will see a black smudge in the air as it is shattered. Speed is essential for all clay shooting, although the technique varies with the different presentation of the target and according to the rules of the particular type of competition. Sometimes the shooter will have his gun up in the aiming position before he calls for the clay to be released, and this somewhat unnatural performance is inclined to engender scorn on the part of the game shooter, who is apt to forget that clay shooting is a contest played to rules, and that anyone who intends to win must exploit the rules to the utmost; just as the sailing man does when he luffs an opponent trying to overtake him, or lodges a protest against another boat which, in his opinion, interferes with him illegally. Clay shooting rules are thorough and definite and you will have to learn them carefully; in some competitions the gun must not be held at the shoulder before the call of 'Pull' and there is a precise definition of what is the correct 'gun down' position.

[20]

Some of the best clay shots specialise in one type of target, perhaps because they find they are better at it and they have ambitions to win prizes and perhaps be selected for a county or National team, or possibly, on a more humble level, because it is not possible for them to find all the layouts of the different competitions near their home. It is better, however, to try all types of shooting, at any rate initially, for each will improve your technique, give you experience and help your game shooting, which is a desirable end for most shooting men; it is a fact, however, that some clay shots limit themselves to their own 'game' and have no interest in shooting real game such as pheasants and partridges, nor even pigeon or duck or any creature which may be shot for sport and to be eaten. Clay shooting is a specialised business, and if it has no attraction for the shooting man whose great joy is working his gun-dog it has a tremendous appeal to the man who revels in controlling himself physically to perform a very difficult task in the face of stern and unrelenting competition.

Some men do not like performing in public, while others obviously enjoy it. Some good shots are happy enough in a party of friends but their performance will fall off considerably if they are observed by strangers, perhaps the spectators at a Field Trial, or farm labourers watching a covert shoot. To shoot well, either at game or clay pigeon, a Gun must have confidence in himself and, apart from safety precautions, be able to ignore people around him. Shooting clays in public helps to overcome nervousness due to being watched and, even if the novice feels a bit of a fool when he misses many birds he will, with experience and instruction, learn to concentrate hard, his whole being compressed onto the thought of the next clay which is just about to dart out in front of him. Onlookers will be ignored.

Most competitions include a system of handicapping, which

[21]

may be done by distance, or points, or classes. For each method an individual's past performance must be known, just as a golf handicap is based on previous form. With the distance method the shooters stand a specified distance behind the trap, the better shots being further away than the less skilful. Points handicapping involves allotting a number of points, or kills, to each competitor, those with the lowest record of percentage of kills to clays receiving the most points. The class system allots a letter to a shooter according to his average score the previous season, as follows :

Class 'AA'—average score of 94% kills or more.
Class 'A'—average score of between 90% and 94% kills.
Class 'B'—average score of between 85% and 90% kills.
Class 'C'—average score of under 85% kills.

There may also be classes for Novices, Ladies, Veterans (over 65 for Sporting Clays, and over 60 for Down-the-Line), Juniors or Colts (under 18) and for Gamekeepers, clubs such as Hunt Clubs and Gun Clubs, and for Counties and areas like Midlands or South of England. In a Championship meeting the winner is naturally the top scorer, but prizes are also awarded to all classes to whom the meeting is open.

The performance of expert clay shots is pretty staggering, and they have an aura of ruthless efficiency; scoring '100 straight', which means a hundred kills without a miss, is nowadays by no means uncommon. Guns and cartridges are usually different from those used for game shooting and the technique includes much more aiming than is allowable in normal shooting. One uses the term 'normal' in no disparagement to the clay shooters but only in the sense that it is surely more 'normal' to shoot something alive which may subsequently be eaten. It is axiomatic of clay shooting that the exponents know when their targets will appear and, within fairly strict limits, what direction they will take. For these reasons they can adopt preparatory positions quite unsuited for ordinary shooting but absolutely necessary if they are to take their shot within that first split second after the clay leaves the trap. It may be called trick shooting but no one denies that it is a specialised performance and exceptional techniques are necessary for the highest success at any sport.

Examples of averages made by first-class shots in England during recent years are: at Down-the-Line, for 3,000 birds, 98%; at Skeet, for 1,275 birds, 95%; at Olympic Trench, for 1,975 birds, 94%. Appendix 'C' gives some details of shooting records and past winners of Championships.

CHAPTER TWO

GUNS AND CARTRIDGES

THERE are many types and sizes of shotgun available and, while the normal game gun is a 12-bore, smaller guns (16-bore, 20-bore) are used by those who want something lighter, and bigger guns (10-bore, 8-bore) by wildfowlers whose main quarry is geese. But for clay shooting the 12-bore with $2\frac{1}{2}$-inch chambers may be regarded as the standard since it delivers a sufficiently large amount of shot at the ranges experienced and larger bores are now barred by the rules. Some clay shooters, however, prefer a gun chambered to take $2\frac{3}{4}$-inch cartridges, particularly for Olympic Trench shooting.

A side-by-side double-barrelled game gun is perfectly adequate for 'Sporting Clays' (see Chapter 8) and the owner of such a gun should not be deterred from trying more specialised clay shooting such as Down-The-Line or Skeet. He will, however, soon see that most of the experienced clay shots use something different and the main reason is that with normal game shooting the technique is to watch the target, a flying bird, and point the gun at it with the left arm whereas in clay shooting the process is much more deliberate and the gun is aimed, at a point in space where the target is expected; one barrel with a prominent rib above it assists the eye in its aim.

The Over-and-under gun, in which one barrel is on top of the other instead of the two being side by side, is probably the most popular clay shooting gun, at any rate in England. These guns are usually expensive and they are heavier than a conventional double-barrelled gun but they find considerable favour with trap-shooters; they often have a single trigger and a selector in the safety catch which permits either barrel to be fired first; normally they are bored with the lower barrel having less choke than the upper, so that the lower is fired first and thus some people call them under-and-over guns, rather than over-and-under. It is claimed that the recoil on these guns is less upsetting to the user because the lower barrel, which is the one most often used, is set further down than is the case with side-to-side barrels, and therefore the thrust of its recoil acts in a lower plane through the stock and more nearly into the centre of the butt plate.

If the clay shooter wants to sight along the top of one barrel, why should he not use a single-barrelled gun? He certainly can, as long as it is capable of firing more than one cartridge, and so he may choose a repeater. One of the best, if you can handle it, is the pump gun on which the fired cartridge case is ejected by pulling back the fore-end which also recocks the gun; pushing the fore-end forward loads another cartridge. This action of the shooter's left hand can pull the muzzle off the line of flight of the target and consequently it is not an easy gun for the inexperienced, although many Americans use pump guns successfully. This may be due to the fact that most American sportsmen have grown up with repeaters: after the American civil war, in which repeating rifles were developed considerably, a demand arose for repeating shotguns to deal with the large amount of game available. By the beginning of this century inexpensive repeaters were common in the United States and now several different types are available in Europe. Another form of manually-operated repeater is the bolt-action gun which has

[25]

somewhat the appearance of a rifle; the need to operate the bolt makes the rate of fire too slow for 'Doubles', when two clay targets are presented at the same time. Another disadvantage of most cheap, mass-produced repeaters is that they are nearly always chambered for $2\frac{3}{4}$-inch cartridges, and consequently they have to be made heavier than they need be were they to be used only for the standard $2\frac{1}{2}$-in. cartridge.

Two other types of single barrel repeater are the recoil operated and the gas operated; these are usually poorly balanced and they are more difficult than a double-barrelled weapon to hold steady for a quickly taken second shot, until the user has had a good deal of practice. All automatic guns include more complicated firing mechanism than is found in a conventional gun and they are therefore more prone to failure, owing perhaps to a small spring breaking; subsequent repairs are apt to be more difficult and expensive. Repeaters also tend to be less safe because the barrels cannot be dropped into an open position like a double-barrelled side-by-side or over-and-under; this open position confirms to everyone interested that the gun is unloaded and in the sporting field it enables the user to check that his barrels are free from obstruction such as mud or snow.

The main parts of a gun are shown on Plate 1. The rib of a clay shooting gun is usually raised higher than on a game gun, is serrated to prevent light reflection and may be ventilated; the ventilation holes are said to obviate a mirage effect due to warm air rising off a hot barrel, as may occur after some fairly intensive shooting on a warm summer day.

On a standard gun the fore-end is primarily a locking piece to hold together the barrels and action and it is not designed to accommodate the shooter's left hand. Often, in fact, a man with a reasonably long reach will have his fingers on the metal of the barrels, beyond the fore-end, at the moment of

[26]

firing, and in mounting the gun he will let the barrels slide through his fingers and only grip with his left hand as he takes the shot. The clay shooter likes to grasp his gun firmly before he shoots but he does not want his left arm considerably bent with the elbow pointing down like a rifle marksman; therefore he demands a long fore-end on his gun which is designed to be gripped in the left hand, and one version of this is called the 'Beaver tail' fore-end, because of its resemblance to the flattened round tail of a beaver. Any form of enlarged fore-end prevents the user from burning his hand on hot barrels but it also adds weight to the gun; by fixing the position of the left hand it can hamper good style in game shooting but it is an advantage for trap shooting.

The length of the barrels of a gun is largely a matter of individual taste, partly determined by physical build. 28 inches is often regarded as a standard length but 30 inches is quite suitable for a reasonably tall man, and the longer barrels tend to make for steadier shooting, particularly at greater ranges. Barrels may be chambered for $2\frac{3}{4}$-inch or even 3-inch cartridges but there is little point in getting a clay shooting gun which can fire these bigger cartridges because the rules normally limit the shot load to $1\frac{1}{8}$-oz. which can be used in the standard $2\frac{1}{2}$-inch cartridge.

The muzzle end of a barrel is usually slightly constricted inside in order to squeeze together the shot charge and so improve the pattern; this is called 'choke', the smallest amount being described as improved cylinder, and larger amounts as $\frac{1}{2}$ or $\frac{3}{4}$ or full choke. For Skeet, where the clays are shot at fairly short range, improved cylinder in both barrels would be suitable, whereas for Down-The-Line a greater degree of choke is called for, perhaps $\frac{1}{2}$ and full, particularly for the second barrel at a small target more or less flat and presenting not much more than its edge to the shooter, and going away from him at high speed. A distinct advantage of a double-barrelled gun is that it offers the immediate choice of two differing degrees of choke; this cannot obtain with single-barrelled guns many of which are somewhat over choked, with the result that their pattern is so tight at about 20 yards that the shooter is at a disadvantage and can easily miss his target. It is of course, a simple matter to have such a barrel bored out so that some of the choke is removed. It is also possible to fit onto the end of the barrel an extension tube which incorporate a fixed degree of choke, or a more advanced type which can be adjusted to give varying degrees of choke. Yet a third sort of variable choke is automatic in that the shock of firing the first shot moves a controlling ring and imposes a greater amount of choke for the second shot. Some of these choke attachments incorporate muzzle-brakes, sometimes called recoil eliminators, and it is worth remembering that such gadgets are normally not permitted by clay shooting rules, at any rate for Down-The-Line shooting; one of the reasons is that they create a sideways blast effect which is not at all pleasant for anyone standing to the side of the user.

Before leaving the subject, mention should be made of an expensive but satisfactory way of obtaining a wide choice of choke variations on a double-barrelled gun, and this is by having two sets of barrels. One set of barrels will be fairly open bored and the other will have more choke. Both must be correctly balanced so that when shooting the user is unaware of which set is on the gun, but he will be using the same stock all the time and he will also experience the same trigger pulls to which he is accustomed.

An incorrect trigger pull is definitely a handicap to good shooting; it should be about $3\frac{1}{2}$ lb. for the right barrel and $4\frac{1}{2}$ lb. for the left on a game gun, and on a specialised gun for clays it is worth testing the pull and experimenting to find a good, crisp feel which suits the owner. Some double-barrelled guns have only a single trigger which is not an advantage unless it is possible to select which barrel will be fired first. Even then the single trigger mechanism is complicated and liable to failure unless carefully looked after; many shooting men regard this feature on a gun as little more than a sales 'gimmick'. Some Continental guns even have two triggers, but with the rear one operating both barrels if required.

Associated with trigger pulling is the grip of the right hand on the small of the butt. For two triggers this part of the gun should be straight, as on most game guns, because the hand can then move more easily to enable the forefinger to reach onto the left trigger. Sometimes the underneath of the stock has a protuberance forming what is called a 'pistol grip' and this provides a hold for the thumb and fingers when using a single trigger; hence most single barrel guns have a pistol grip or more correctly, in most cases, a half pistol grip, the 'half pistol' having a less pronounced bump. This does help the hold of the right hand to remain constant while the forefinger is released on the trigger before taking the second shot. A full pistol grip may help if there is some deformity of the hand but for the average man it may be too much of a good thing and cause the wrist to ache when doing a lot of continuous competition shooting. (Plate 2.)

The lock is the heart of a gun and the most common type is called a box lock; it is strong and adequate for most people, but if you can afford a side lock you will be able to obtain finer adjustment of trigger pulls and you will have a more beautiful looking gun. The side lock also incorporates an intercepting safety stop to prevent the gun firing if it suffers a sudden jar such as being dropped; the safety catch alone, be it noted, may well not prevent the tumbler from being released and firing the cartridge.

So, if you are a comparative newcomer to clay shooting and you are wondering what sort of gun you ought to buy, you have quite a problem on your hands. You must decide for what purpose, primarily, the gun is going to be used. Do you want it for game shooting as well? If so a double-barrelled game gun would suit but if you are going into the clay busting business seriously you will scarcely be content with anything less than an over-and-under and two sets of barrels. You will have to decide whether your money is best invested in a new gun or a second-hand one, an English made gun or a cheaper foreign one. Good second-hand guns are available but should be bought only from a reputable dealer, preferably a member of the Gun Trade Association. Never buy an old gun from a stranger without testing it and offering it for inspection by a qualified gunsmith; old barrels may be lapped to remove pitting and when this is carried to excess they become 'out of proof'. Nitro-proofing involves submitting gun barrels to very great pressures, as a safety precaution, and no gun may legally be sold in Great Britain unless it is 'in proof'. (See Appendix 'D', paragraph 13, 14, 15). If you buy an automatic, probably a foreign one, because it is cheap remember that it will generally be more difficult to clean and repair, and for normal shooting it is not so easily carried and will be noisy to load and unload. It will also, most likely, be far from handsome. Nevertheless, such a gun can be adequately functional as a start to clay shooting. Before paying for a type of gun different from that to which you are accustomed you would do well to try several shots with it to see if you like it, and to find out whether that type suits you.

On cartridges the clay shooter is more restricted than the game shooter owing to the competition rules. You should use good cartridges and not try to economise with something cheap; crimp closure, by doing away with the over shot wad,

gives a better pattern than the now old-fashioned rolled turn-
over at the front end. You need not worry initially about the
patterns of different shot sizes because you will probably
accept size 7 as a standard, but if you want to investigate the
denser pattern from No. 8 shot do it properly, and the best
way is on the pattern plate at the Shooting School when you
have your gun fitted. Do not try to reach a decision after one
shot at a newspaper on a barn door some unmeasured distance away. You will find most clay shooters content to use
the standard 'Trap load' cartridges which have $1\frac{1}{8}$ oz. of shot
and a fairly slow burning powder. Do not be persuaded to
use 'high velocity' cartridges in the belief that the shot will
travel so much quicker that the target will be easier to hit; the
difference from standard in the striking velocity is usually
small and if it was very much greater it could have the effect
of a pellet making a small hole in the clay without breaking
it. More will be said about high velocity cartridges in
Chapter 6.

A shotgun should be correctly fitted to its user. Apart from
having a gun made for you, it is quite possible to obtain a
good fit by taking your gun to a shooting school where the
correct measurements can be found by the instructor watching you shoot with an adjustable try-gun. You can make a
rough test at home by throwing up the gun at a few aiming
marks, keeping both eyes open, and then closing the left eye
to check where the gun is pointing. Too much bend in the
stock results in the gun pointing low, while a high point of
aim is caused by too little bend. The amount by which the
gun points to left or right of the aiming mark is determined
by the cast-off, which is a displacement of the butt sideways
so that it is not quite in line with the barrels. This is done to
compensate for the fact that the shooter's shoulder, support-
ing the butt, is displaced to the side of his eyes. If the whole

stock is too short it will not bed properly into your shoulder and the recoil of firing will be painful; too long a stock will probably catch in your clothing as you mount the gun and will also make it difficult for you to reach the triggers. The position of the eye as it looks along the barrel is important too, and if you aim at the reflection of your own eye in a mirror you should see the whole eye exactly above the gun rib. If the eye is partly obscured or if some of your right cheek is showing the gun is not fitting properly. (Plate 10.)

At the shooting school you will fire several shots at the pattern plate, which is usually steel and covered with whitewash so that the impressions of the pellets can be easily seen. As well as testing your accuracy this will show the pattern thrown by your gun and cartridges at a known range. After using your own gun you will fire the adjustable try-gun and the instructor will alter it until he has made you shoot correctly with it. All the measurements can be given to the gunsmith who is going to alter your gun, and the instructor should also check such details as the height of the comb, which should bring the stock comfortably against your cheek; this height may be incorrect initially if your neck is a little longer or shorter than average. The position of your right hand on the small of the butt should enable you comfortably to reach the triggers with the pad of your forefinger, keeping your other fingers clear of the rear of the trigger guard, and you must also be able easily to reach the safety catch.

Much can be done to improve the fit of a ready-made gun and the trouble taken is always worth while if you want to shoot seriously.

Having acquired the best gun you can afford and of the type most suitable to your purpose you may as well take a little interest in your clothes. For clay shooters this subject is much less bound by tradition and shot through with con-

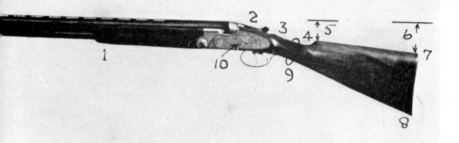

1. The parts of a gun. This is a 12 bore under-and-over with raised ventilated rib; the ends of the barrels are not included in the picture.
1. Fore-end. 2. Top Lever. 3. Safety catch. 4. Comb. 5. Drop, or bend, at comb. 6. Drop at heel. 7. Heel, or bump, of butt. 8. Toe of butt. 9. Small of the butt, or grip, or hand. 10. Lock, in this case a side lock.

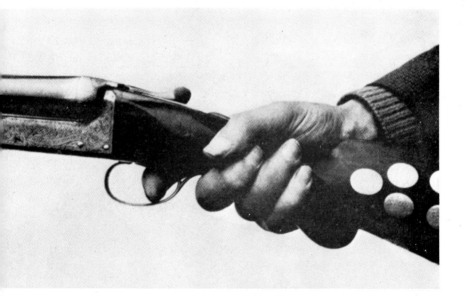

2. The finger on the trigger. A firm hold with the right hand, pad of the forefinger on the single trigger; the gun has a half pistol grip.

3. Dress. A Skeet squad demonstrates a variety of dress and a preference for automatics, some with variable chokes.

troversy than it is among those who attend important covert shoots, or camouflage themselves from sharp-eyed pigeon, or try to keep warm lying in the mud in a bitter wind while flighting wildfowl, but even so a tip or two for the novice will do no harm. You will soon notice a kind of uniform, either club blazers with breast pocket badges, or a light specially-made-for-the-job kind of jacket made of gaberdine or nylon, although many shooters are happy in loose-fitting sweaters. (Plate 3.) Most serious clay shooting takes place in the summer, and when it is hot you should beware of trying to shoot in shirtsleeves if your gun was fitted when you had on a thick tweed jacket. A cap with a long peak is useful to protect the eyes and many shooters use sunglasses of various tints, polaroid glasses being the best to combat glare. Shoes present no problem, for one great advantage the clay shooter has over the game shot is that he always stands on a firm, level platform. For shooting in the rain a loose nylon mackintosh is acceptable; it is sensible to try to keep dry because discomfort does not help straight shooting. Various club events are held throughout the year and sometimes in weather that calls for coats, gloves and gumboots. It is worth while giving some thought to the problem of what to wear, and still be able to shoot, in bad weather and it is wise to remember that clay shooting can be a very cold business. The layouts are usually on an exposed site and they are arranged so that they face to the north; this helps to keep the sun out of our eyes in the summer but it places us right in the path of a cold nor'-easter in the winter.

To protect your gun you should have a gun case in which it may be packed for travelling; and a gun cupboard with a glass front is an admirable piece of furniture at home, especially if you have more than one gun. In the cupboard guns may be stored assembled in one piece, and they can easily be taken out for inspection and handled; the more the learner shot handles his gun the better, so that he gets used to it, and so that he is more inclined to do practice mounting exercises, as described in Chapter 9. The bottom part of the cupboard should consist of drawers or shelves for storing cartridges and cleaning materials.

Gun cleaning is much simpler now, since the introduction of cartridges with non-corrosive primers and impregnated wads which partially clean the weapon each time it is fired. Nonetheless a few hints may be worth while:

1. Have two cleaning rods, one for the cleaning rag or brush and one for the oily mop used for finally oiling the barrels after cleaning.

2. Push small bits of rolled-up newspaper through the barrels in the first place, thus removing the main dirt and prolonging the life of the cleaning rag.

3. Instead of using ordinary rag or tow for cleaning the barrels try the special Shotgun Patches made by Parker Hale; these are made the right size according to bore and so save time, just as 'Four-by-Two' flannelette is the correct size for cleaning a .303 rifle.

4. Have a phosphor bronze brush for stubborn bits of fouling.

5. Use a rust-preventing oil, such as 'Young's .303 cleaner'.

6. Use a feather, the quill for cleaning round and under the extractors and the soft end for lightly oiling the triggers, base of the rib etc. A fairly stiff feather such as that from a pigeon's tail is better than a soft one like a pheasant's.

7. If the gun is very wet after rain stand it on its muzzles to drain the water away down the barrels and not back into the action. Use blotting paper for drying such

[36]

places as the base of the rib where it joins the barrels. Examine the gun the day after cleaning to see if there is any sweating, which will need wiping and re-oiling. After a wet day, the locks of a side-lock gun can be removed, or the bottom plate of a boxlock, and water mopped out with a clean, cotton rag. The screwdriver must fit the screw heads accurately, which probably means that it will need filing, in order to enter the fine slots. Many gunsmiths, however, consider that un-skilled owners would do less harm to their guns, if they did *not* attempt to take them to bits!

Another point of gun cleaning concerns the stock. It should be wiped clean of mud and have some linseed oil rubbed in as a preservative; if you want to raise a bit more of a shine on the stock use 'artist's quality' linseed oil mixed with about a third as much turpentine. Do not smother the wood with the gun oil which can cause it to swell and interfere danger-ously with the working of the lock, as explained in Chapter 3.

After shooting, wipe the gun over, push a patch through each barrel, and then clean and examine it thoroughly when you get home. You will meet cheerful souls who will tell you that with modern cartridges there is hardly any need to clean a gun at all, and that certainly no harm will be done if you postpone the job a day; but a man who has a care for his gun, who can take pleasure in the beauty of its appear-ance and enjoy looking after it properly, will surely find his reward in the possession of an instrument, almost a com-panion, that will provide him with much enjoyment and never let him down unexpectedly. (Plate 4.)

Incidentally, from 1st May, 1968, it became law that a certificate, issued by the police, is required by anyone who possesses, purchases or acquires, a shotgun.

CHAPTER THREE

SHOTGUN HANDLING
AND SHOOTING

Many youngsters come to shotgun shooting by way of the rifle, probably a .177 airgun and then, maybe, a .22 used at rabbits or pigeon and also as a target weapon. Sometimes the newcomer's attitude to the shotgun is one of undue confidence that it must be easy to use because it fires 'spread shot' which can cover a multitude of errors, but this idea is very far from the truth. Highly accurate rifle shooting is by no means easy but the marksman does have plenty of time: to adopt a comfortable position, to make sure the butt is correctly in the right place against his shoulder, to line up his sights, keep steady, hold his breath and carefully squeeze the trigger. His target remains stationary and although there are outside elements, such as wind, to be considered, particularly at long ranges, his approach to each shot is pretty much the same. The shotgunner's targets are moving, usually fast, and in different directions, at varying angles and speeds and ranges, and all these factors have to be dealt with at once, together with foot and body movements and the correct mounting of the gun to the shoulder.

In order to explain the basic principles of using a shotgun we will first consider the shooting of a bird in flight and then work out how to deal with the artificial, a clay 'bird', under the special conditions imposed by competitive shooting.

The fundamental rule is that when the bird is seen, and

accepted as being in range, the gun must not be flung up to the shoulder and the barrels waved across the sky, chasing after the bird until the shooter decides he had better pull the trigger soon or his quarry will have departed out of range. But that is what often does happen when the uninstructed novice first gets his hands on a shotgun. Quite likely he soon realises that the birds he is trying to shoot really are moving fast so he tries to quicken up his drill, whips the gun up, fires 'Bang! Bang!' and is more than a little sad to see that he has missed; although, in actual fact, he has hit what his gun was aimed at, which was a piece of sky a couple of yards behind his target. The correct procedure is to hold the gun with the butt down and the muzzles out in front, pointing up at about 45°, and to move the left hand so as to keep the muzzles between the bird and your eyes; the muzzles are then held on the line of flight all the time while the gun is mounted, and the shot is taken as mounting is completed and the barrels come into line where your eyes are looking. (Plate 9.) Swinging the gun ahead of the bird, giving it forward allowance, or lead, will be explained later; at the moment you should concentrate on handling your gun correctly and safely, and understanding how to place it in the correct position for shooting. Now let us examine the correct way to mount the gun, from the beginning.

Good gun mounting requires a correct stance, and grip, and aim and a stylish technique to co-ordinate all the movements. If you can master the several actions in correct mounting you will be able to shoot reasonably well with any gun under any circumstances but for top performance and for quick shooting, whether at game or clays, a properly fitted gun is essential. A made-to-measure gun, however, will not be of much help if the man behind has not learnt how to handle it.

The stance should be comfortable and although it may vary a little according to the build of the shooter, the feet ought to be fairly close together, and the general attitude is that of a half turn to the right front. Common faults are feet too far apart and the right foot nearly alongside the left so that the shooter's chest is almost facing his target instead of being at an angle of about 45° to the line of fire. (Plates 5, 6.) Nearly all the weight is on the left foot, the right heel is just clear of the ground and a slight forward lean induces a feeling of mild resistances in the left hip; it is not a tension, for the whole body from the hips up must be able to rotate right or left for slightly more than a right angle without the feet being moved. The left knee is not bent and it is the only joint that is kept stiff during the rotating movements.

This swinging from side to side is worth practising with the arms held out horizontally in front of you, palms facing down keeping the left hand nearly opposite the right; this is more difficult when pivoting to the left but that does not matter since, when shooting, the left arm is in front of the right as your chest remains obliquely to your front. Then you can practise pivoting while holding the gun and this ought to impress on you how you can get your body round to face the target and that it is wrong to move your arm across your body and turn your head; see Figure I for correct stance.

Balance should remain perfect throughout these rotational movements and the gun barrels must stay level, which they will do if body and shoulders remain square, but any swaying of the body will drop a shoulder. It is not correct to shift the weight to the right foot and raise the left heel when swinging to the right because this will cause the right shoulder to drop and so will cant the barrels sideways, and make the shot miss low. In clay shooting one can adopt this perfect foot position as one is always standing on level ground or even

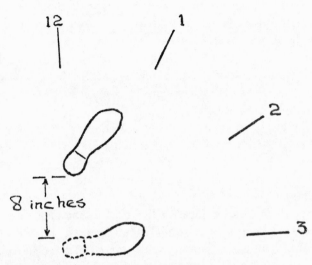

FIG. I. – STANCE
The correct position for the feet, the shooter's front being towards
twelve o'clock.

on concrete slabs so that the footwork necessary for game
shooting, where one is standing on uneven ground and slopes,
does not arise; in this respect Clay shooting is easier than
game. (Plates 11, 12, 13, 14.)

The gun should be gripped firmly with the right hand at
the small of the butt, sometimes called 'grip' or 'hand'. It is
a good solid hold which could raise the gun to the shoulder
without using the left hand at all. The left hand has an
entirely different sort of grip which varies from a loose hold
through which the gun can slide to a firm grip between fingers
and thumb, but not using the palm of the hand to grasp the
gun.

Before arranging the position of the left hand on the gun
let us consider the vital function of that hand in aiming the
gun. Try a little experiment: stick your left hand out in

[41]

front of you and point at any object with the forefinger. There is an automatic co-ordination between eye and finger and both are concentrated on the same object. Now turn over the palm of your left hand and extend the thumb straight out and slightly to the left. Your left hand and arm are now pretty well in the correct position for holding and pointing a game gun.

The left hand is always thrust out at your target. Its hold initially, from wherever it was on the gun while you were at rest, is light and the barrels can slide through it; this hand moves first in mounting the gun and it puts the muzzles on the target and holds them there while the butt is down. Then, as the right hand brings up the butt to the shoulder and cheek, the barrels slide through the fingers of the left hand which grips them when the butt is locked into the shoulder; the attitude of the left hand is with the thumb lying straight along the left barrel, the first finger running up between and underneath the two barrels, pointing, and the three remaining fingers gripping the right barrel along its side. There should be no finger or thumb over the top of either barrel and no weight in the palm of the hand.

If the thumb comes over the left barrel your line of sight, instead of running straight up the centre of the barrels over the rib, will be deflected up the right barrel, which means that the barrels are sighted slightly to the right and you will miss on that side; should the fingers appear over the right barrel the converse applies and the shot misses to the left.

This description of the left hand lying under the barrels with the forefinger extended applies to the normal double-barrelled game gun. On a clay shooting gun having an enlarged fore-end designed to be grasped in the left hand the procedure is necessarily a little different. With the barrels pointing down, and slightly across the body, you should grasp the fore-end between fingers and thumb at the place where you intend it to be when the gun is mounted, and this place must always be the same for every shot. Exactly how you hold the fore-end depends on its size and the length of your arms; some shooters hold a pump gun with the left fore-finger curled round the front of the fore-end and that is a good position but others may not be able to reach so far out. Care must still be taken to see that fingers and thumb do not intrude over the top of the barrel and it is important that the position of gripping is always the same. (Plate 7, 8.)

Beginners nearly always hold a gun with the left hand too far back, and if they also adopt a tight grip and have fingers or thumb on top of the barrels they tend to try to look over the top so that sighting becomes wildly erratic. There is no specific position along the barrels where the left hand must be positioned but a straight or very nearly straight arm is recommended since it gives better balance for the gun, keeps the muzzles up and is the natural position for pointing. The closer grip with a bent left elbow is usually adopted because the shooter has graduated to the shotgun from the rifle and thinks in terms of a tight hold and aiming, instead of a freely moving left arm and pointing.

Now, with your stance correct and a knowledge of how to grip the gun you will need to practise mounting, which calls for co-ordination of eye and brain with movements of arms and body, and perhaps feet as well. Mounting starts when the bird is first seen (we are still considering a bird and not a clay): the correct stance is taken, with the left foot point-ing at about 1 o'clock from the target; the left hand pushes out the barrels towards the bird so that you can watch it over the muzzles, and as the bird swings to either side of you so does your body pivot and allow the muzzles to stay on; at this stage the stock is lying along the lower forearm, with

[43]

the butt by your elbow; as the right hand then brings up the butt the left arm thrusts out, gripping the barrels, and for a fraction of a second the gun is at eye level and the butt is just touching the shoulder but not bedded firmly against it, and at this critical moment your shoulder comes forward to meet the butt; as the butt comes hard into the shoulder you squeeze the trigger. During the whole movement your body is pivoting as required by the movement of the bird and your gun muzzles are swinging with it and being raised by the left hand to keep them on target.

The mounting of the gun is a deliberate, smooth and comparatively slow movement and the body is relaxed until the instant of firing. As the gun meets the shoulder the left arm is pulling it forward and this, combined with the tight grip of the right hand and the thrust forward of the shoulder, results in practically no recoil being felt. The cheek must be bedded closely on the stock and the head held normally erect, not bent down to get the eye low nor bent back in instinctive fear of the shock of discharge. As the gun is fired the left knee is stiff and the shoulder and neck muscles are tensed but the hips remain fluid and continue the swing of body and gun barrels. Both elbows should be in a natural midway position, not pointing down to the ground and not stuck out horizontally. Common mistakes with beginners are to relax their grip at the moment of firing, to draw away their heads or shoulders and to flinch, all of which, besides ensuring a miss, result in the recoil giving them a blow on the shoulder or even on the upper biceps when the butt has slipped; sometimes a smack in the mouth from the top of the stock can also be caused in this way. Have no fear when you fire a gun; hold it firmly, be determined to master it and have confidence that you are going to point it in the right direction and pull the trigger exactly when you want to.

[44]

One talks of mounting a gun slowly but it is really the deliberation that needs emphasising. If you watch a good shot in action he appears to be slow because he is precise and his movements are not hasty and jerked. Your mounting must also be slow but it must finish with a snap; you are leaning forward a bit as you mount the gun, you keep your eye unwaveringly on the target but when your gun is up you fire at once, with no dawdling about waving your gun across the sky in pursuit of your bird. If you see a shooter hanging in the aim like that with his gun muzzles following a bird you can be practically certain he is going to miss. It is very bad style and even if its followers sometimes score a hit they really scarcely deserve to.

Basically, then, gun mounting consists of :

1. Eye picks up bird and body pivots with it.
2. Left hand puts muzzle on, butt still down.
3. Right hand brings up butt slowly, while body and left hand keep muzzle on line of flight.
4. Shoulder comes into butt and gun is fired.

Remember that this explanation is of the way to mount a gun to shoot a live bird, while you are standing behind a hedge, perhaps, and watching a pigeon approach. But you may have seen some trapshooting and you will say 'But the chaps I saw already had their guns up at their shoulders before ever the clay was released from the trap. What has gun mounting, as you describe it, got to do with that?'— The answer is that the gun always has to be mounted and if there is lots of time to do so, as in Down-The-Line shooting, that is a bonus; any variations from the game shooting method will be discussed in Chapter 4 but in order for you to assimilate the idea of how a shotgun is pointed in the right direction, it is better for you to understand and practise the

[45]

movements of gun mounting described in this Chapter. We will now examine some other points which occur in handling and which can affect safety and efficiency.

When should you put the safety catch to the firing position? Basically, the answer is 'Only just before the trigger is pulled'. You should certainly not have the safety catch off while you are waiting to shoot. The correct time to push forward the safety slide is as you prepare for your shot and this means that three things happen simultaneously.

1. Weight on the left foot in the direction of the bird.
2. Muzzle in line with the bird, stock still down along the forearm.
3. Safety slide pushed forward.

You then carry on mounting the gun and take the shot but, if for any reason you do not shoot, your immediate re-action as you lower the gun must be to push the slide back to 'Safe'. While you are in the ready position, and you are pushing the safety catch off, it is most important that your right forefinger should be along the trigger guard and it must not move onto the trigger until the next stage when you bring the butt to your shoulder. If you allow your finger to stray onto the trigger too soon there is every possibility that the action of pushing off the safety catch with your thumb will result in a corresponding movement back of your finger, and the gun will go off. Besides being potentially dangerous to others this can result in the top lever jabbing back on recoil and cutting the top of your thumb. To avoid risk of this injury the thumb should be trained to flick back to the side of the grip immediately it has operated the safety catch.

It is sometimes advocated that the safety catch should be pushed off as the gun is mounted, but this can be dangerous because the thumb may again be caught by the top lever if

[46]

the gun is fired a little too quickly; it can also be frustrating if the thumb is a bit slow and the finger tries to pull the trigger before the thumb has managed to work the catch. So play safe and set the safety catch for firing as you prepare for a shot, and remember to keep your trigger finger along the guard.

Safety is the most important element of shooting. We all think we are safe, just as we all think we are good car drivers and that when an accident occurs it is the other fellow who is to blame. But a great many shooting men are unsafe at some time or another and although they know that a gun, even an unloaded one, should never be pointed at anyone they become careless in their handling and allow their gun muzzles to point at someone else's feet, or at his dog. A gun held under the upper arm and over the forearm should be 'broken' so that everyone can see that it is unloaded. If you have a single barrelled automatic which cannot be 'broken' you ought never to carry it under your arm when in the company of others. Put it over your shoulder, trigger uppermost and muzzle well up in the air. Never carry a gun with your arm down by your side, holding the gun at its point of balance, with the barrel horizontal. Nor should you hold a gun with both hands, the arms vertically down in front of the legs; the horizontal barrels are then almost certain to be pointing at your neighbour, but this casual position is often adopted by lazy shooters while waiting for game to appear.

You should always unload a gun before crossing an obstacle such as a ditch or a fence and before putting it in a car or bringing it into a house. In fact, when you walk back to your car after shooting open the gun and look to see that it is unloaded even though you *know* you unloaded it some time beforehand. More accidents are caused by guns believed to be unloaded than by those whose owners knew them to be loaded. Safe gun handling should become an automatic drill, so that whenever you pick up a gun the first thing you do is to check that it is not loaded; so that you never pass a gun to anyone else without showing him that it is unloaded; so that you always unload immediately after shooting is finished, whether game or clays be the object; and so that you simply cannot hold a gun by its muzzle and pull it towards you, as when crawling through a wire fence or taking the gun out of a car. (Plate 15, 16.)

Remember that a shotgun can throw its pellets for two or three hundred yards and that even at that extreme range they could damage an eye. And the pressure inside the barrels when the cartridge fires is about $2\frac{3}{4}$ tons per square inch, so if you buy a second-hand gun have it tested by a proper gunsmith, preferably before paying the price; old barrels are sometimes bored out to remove pitting and this weakens them so that the gun could burst.

Do not shoot unless you can see what lies beyond your target. Do not lean a gun upright against a wall or a car; it can easily be knocked over, perhaps by a dog; it could go off if it was loaded and a knock will almost certainly dent the barrels. One small dent will not do much harm, although it ought to be removed as soon as possible, but several will interfere with the shot pattern and also cause undue pressure to be set up in the barrel which could be the cause of a burst.

The Safety Catch on a gun needs understanding, particularly as the very name is misleading and on many guns, when the slide is back, the word 'Safe' is visible. The operation of this slide locks the triggers; no more. It does not hold the action of the lock in any way and on an old gun the nose of the trigger sear is often worn so that a sudden jolt could cause it to slip off the tumbler; this is an internal hammer under pressure from the mainspring of the lock, and when freed it strikes the cartridge cap and fires the gun. The stock of an old gun may be swollen or warped and it could prevent the sear engaging properly with the tumbler so that the jar of closing the gun would cause the tumbler to slip free and fire it. The same fault may cause the second barrel to go off unexpectedly when the first one is fired.

The trigger lock, or so called Safety Catch, is usually brought into play by the movement of the action lever when the gun is opened and this is called 'Automatic Safety'. If the gun is not so fitted the safety slide has to be moved back by hand after the gun has been closed; this is not satisfactory and is potentially dangerous and it is a point to watch when buying an old gun or one of the new cheap ones.

At clay shoots, where many people are carrying guns and where there are also a good many onlookers, it is most important that you are always safe, so your gun must never be loaded unless you are on the firing-line, and never before the referee says 'Line Ready' in Down-The-Line, or tells you to go to your shooting station in Sporting events or Skeet. At all times, whether loaded or otherwise, keep your gun pointing forward, away from other competitors and spectators.

To load a gun which can be broken at the breech, open the gun, put in the cartridges and close it by bringing the butt up to the barrels, with the muzzle still pointing down, not by raising the barrels to the horizontal. With a pump gun or automatic, keep the barrel pointing down as you load and until you start your preparation for the shot. Remember that only two cartridges may be loaded even though your repeater is capable of taking more.

After loading, prepare for the shot by bringing the muzzle up into the line of sight where you are looking for your target to appear, with the butt still down; push the safety catch off, keeping the forefinger off the trigger. If something goes

[49]

wrong with the trap or the clay breaks as it is thrown, lower your gun and put the safety catch on again. Never turn round for any reason whatsoever with a cartridge in the chamber and always make sure you are unloaded as you retire from your firing mark; leave your gun open if you are using a drop barrel type, and if you have an automatic look and see that the breech is open. Do not 'know' that you loaded only two cartridges, two have come out and therefore the gun must be empty; only by seeing an open breech and empty chamber can you be certain that the gun is safe to carry around. And when carrying any gun, away from the firing point, if you do not wish to keep the breech open, because it is raining perhaps, carry it on your shoulder, muzzles up, and not over your arm with the barrel pointing at other people's legs.

Another important little movement in gun handling is that of the finger on the trigger. The pull should be practically unnoticed, which means that when the brain says 'Fire!' the forefinger contracts on the trigger and the shooter is immediately aware that the gun has gone off. This may all sound obvious but the point is that for such a satisfactory state of affairs to occur the weight of the trigger pulls must be correct. The subject was mentioned briefly in Chapter 2 when standard trigger pulls were given as about $3\frac{1}{2}$ and $4\frac{1}{2}$ lb., the second trigger pull always being a bit heavier than the first because its position allows the finger to obtain greater leverage so that it feels correspondingly lighter, and also because the movement onto the second trigger is usually harsher and quicker than onto the first. Trigger pulls can work out of adjustment and they can be wrong in newly acquired second-hand guns, and so you can appreciate that this is a point to watch, or at least to be aware of, because although trigger troubles are not very common they can be increasingly

4. Giving the gun a thorough clean in the gunroom.

5.
A bad aiming position weight back on right foot, body turned too much to front, left hand too far back, fingers over top of barrels, left elbow down in rifle shooting manner.

6.
A good aiming position, feet close together, cheek well onto the stock and a comfortable hold with the left hand.

7. A good grip with the left hand, fore-finger extended. The stance is a little wide but the weight is well forward.

8. Most game shooters prefer to extend their left hand well along the barrels, and this pheasant shooter has a specially made long fore-end on his gun so that he can still hold it with his left hand.

important as the skill of the shooter increases. Too light a trigger pull can result in shots going off too soon, before the shooter is properly on his target, and they are also a source of danger, too heavy a pull may cause the gun to be dragged off its target as the shooter struggles to haul back the triggers.

The weight of a trigger pull should be heavier with a heavy gun than with a light one, although the feel to the user will be the same. Some very good shots with sensitive hands like to have light trigger pulls and they need the best locks for this; only a good side-lock can provide an unvarying and sharp pull as light as about 2 lb. The more skilful shot does develop an increasing awareness of trigger pulls particularly if he uses more than one gun. When different guns are used, for Skeet and Down-The-Line, perhaps, it is essential that the pulls shall be the same, otherwise the user will notice the difference and lose concentration. The average shooting man need not worry much about trigger pulls; they do affect gun handling, but only when the shooter is aware that something feels odd is there any necessity to take action and check the pulls. Adjustment requires care and skill and should be carried out only by a qualified gunsmith.

The balance of any piece of sporting equipment that is held in the hand affects the man who uses it, and fishermen and tennis players, cricketers and golfers all pay attention to the balance of their rods and racquets, bats and clubs. So also is the balance of a gun of interest to a shooter. But do not think 'balance' literally refers to a place on a gun where it can be balanced, see-sawing gently up and down if supported only at that spot. You may meet gun-knowledgeable characters who take your gun, place a finger under the joint pin joining the barrels to the stock and allow the gun to balance there for a moment, unsupported through the rest of its length. According to whether the muzzle or the butt dips down they mutter sagely: 'Well balanced gun, that one', or 'Don't like it, seems heavy in the stock', but these remarks are nonsense. Your gun is correctly balanced for you if it feels right when you mount it.

It is difficult for the novice to know what a right 'feel' of a gun is like, just as the newcomer to tennis has little idea of how the balance of his racquet ought to feel. But a little experience soon gives him the idea. The balance of a gun varies with different people and you can tell whether it is nicely balanced for you by picking it up, holding it loosely in both hands for a moment, and then mounting it. If the muzzle seems to 'ask' to go forward and up, then that gun suits you, but if it feels heavy and clumsy in front and does not 'want' to go where you wish to put it the balance is wrong, for you, but it is not necessarily a badly balanced gun. Your gun must feel right in your hands and if the balance seems easy and pleasant mounting will be helped and shooting will benefit. The balance is affected by the distribution of the weight towards the ends, outside the two places where the hands hold the gun; the greater the proportion of the total weight that can be concentrated here the more the gun will be better balanced and have that desirable quality known as 'fast handling'. Repeaters, especially with choke attachments on the ends of their barrels, are at a disadvantage in this respect. Incidentally, it is possible to have a gun whose 'fast handling' is too much for its user, particularly if he is a large man and his gun is a lightweight with 26-inch barrels. A slower, heavier gun is steadier and more likely to help a good, unchecked swing.

Eyesight controls shotgun shooting in as much as that the whole object of correct gun mounting is to make the gun point where the eye is looking. With most people the right eye is master, but sometimes both eyes take equal control and sometimes the left is the stronger. You can do a simple test to see whether your right eye is the master by extending your right arm to the front and pointing at an object with your forefinger, both eyes being open; now close your left eye and look along your arm and finger as if it was a rifle and you will probably find the finger is still pointing at the object because, although you had both eyes open, the right took control. If, however, your left eye is master eye you will find, when you close it, that your finger seems to be pointing well to the left of your target; now close the right eye and open the left and the finger is pointing true, as you thought you had aimed originally, showing that your left eye took control.

It is normal to shoot with both eyes open because binocular vision allows us to judge ranges and monocular vision does not. There are, however, shooting men who always prefer to shoot with their left eyes closed and sometimes this may be advisable, with reservation. For instance, you may find that you have reasonable success when shooting targets in front, overhead or to the right, but that those coming in on the left are frequently missed. This could be because, whereas your right eye is normally the master eye, the target suddenly appearing to the left is picked up first by your left eye and that this eye 'holds on to' it, directs the muzzles to the wrong place and causes a miss. Such apparently inexplicable misses to the left are not very common but if you do find such a thing happening it is worth consulting a coach at a Shooting School and he will soon diagnose the cause of the trouble. The misses may have nothing to do with eyesight but if they are caused by the left eye taking control there is no remedy in the fit of the gun. The only solution is to dim, or half close the left eye, not when the target is first seen, but as the muzzles are put onto it so that the right eye takes over as the gun is mounted. Partially closing the left eye is sufficient and a complete wink, which might be a bit of a strain, is not necessary. The dimming of the left eye can take place at any time after binocular vision is no longer required, which at clays means just before you call 'Pull!'.

When both eyes are equally strong the gun can have a central vision fitting which entails considerable cast-off of the stock so that the rib appears centrally in front of both eyes. Even with a normal right master-eye it may be necessary to check the fit of a gun as its owner becomes older. Young men see out of the centre of the pupil but with middle-age there comes an increasing tendency to look out of the inner corner of the eye; the slight displacement of the start of the line of sight means that the barrels are pushed over to the left but the shooter is not aware of how, or why, he misses on that side, only that he does. A visit to a Shooting School where the instructor can check alignment of eye and muzzle, can correct this fault by using the try-gun to check cast-off, which will have to be increased. With a little extra cast-off the effects of age can be reduced.

If the left eye is definitely master or if the right has lost its sight there is no reason why shooting should not be done from the left shoulder, except that it may be awkward for the normally right handed man. To shoot from the right shoulder, using the left eye, an across-eyed stock is required; this makes an odd-looking gun which has much exaggerated cast-off but it is a good arrangement for a man who has lost his right eye. In a case where the left eye is master but the right is perfectly good if it could be made to work an across-eyed stock is not worth the trouble, and the better solution is to half-close the left eye as the gun is mounted, as described above.

If you have faulty vision which requires spectacles to

[58]

correct it you may find it advisable to have a special pair for shooting. These should have large lenses, with a shape like a triangle with rounded corners, to give you a good field of view and they can also with advantage have the lower edge of the lenses set a little further away from the face than normal; this will help to keep the line of sight more nearly at right angles through the lenses when you are looking upwards.

As a final comment on gun mounting, you are recommended to try to cultivate a good style. Watch good shots in action and you will see perfect balance, unhurried movements, rhythm and swing and a certain snap as the shot is actually taken; watching such a performance you will feel convinced that the shot has connected with the target without bothering to look and see, but, of course, you must watch the man on the ground and pay no attention to what he is shooting at. Style cannot be perfect every time for, just as the greatest cricket batsmen make mistakes occasionally so do the expert shots sometimes fail to shoot straight. But when your style is right you can feel it; you know your gun muzzles are right on the line of flight, you know just when to pull the trigger and you are so certain of a kill that there is no need to look and see. And the secret of good style is practice in gun mounting.

CHAPTER FOUR

DOWN-THE-LINE

This form of clay pigeon shooting was the first popular shotgun game and it remains the best way of introducing the novice to the sport of competition shooting. Often called 'trapshooting', it helps to develop a sound basic technique because it allows the shooter time to mount his gun properly, and because the unknown angles at which the targets are thrown make his gun handling quick and train his body to swing correctly.

Five competitors, known as a squad, stand 16 yards behind the trap at firing marks numbered 1 to 5, from left to right. See Figure II. The trapper in his shot-proof house puts a clay in the trap and the referee calls 'Line ready'; the first shooter at No. 1 stand loads two cartridges, takes up his shooting stance and says 'Pull!' whereupon the puller, 7 yards behind the line of firing marks, pulls a lever which is connected by a bar through a tube along the ground to the trap; this releases the clay and the shooter fires, using his second barrel if he misses with the first. Then number 2 has his turn and the same procedure follows for each member of the squad, this being repeated until each man has had five clays. On the order of the referee to change, numbers 1, 2, 3 and 4 move one place 'Down the Line' to their right, number 5 comes round to No. 1 firing mark and they all have another five clays in turn; the drill is repeated until all the squad has had five clays at each of the five marks, making a total of 25 and then another squad takes over. In a '100 bird' competition each squad, having shot its first stage of 25 clays, returns to the firing line three more times to make up the total. (Plate 17.)

When the puller has released the trap to send off a clay he pushes his lever forward and this recocks the trap so that it is ready to fire again; all the trapper has to do is to place a clay on the throwing arm. For Down-The-Line competi-

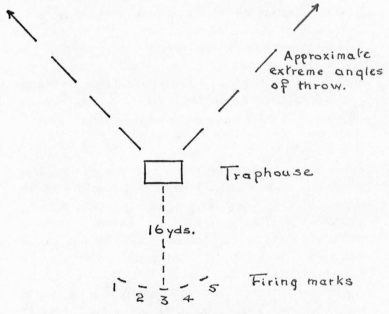

Approximate extreme angles of throw.

Traphouse

16 yds.

Firing marks

1   2   3   4   5

FIG. II. – DOWN-THE-LINE LAYOUT

tions, however, a more advanced trap is used than the simple one for initial instruction, when the trapper himself can alter the direction in which the clay is thrown; the D.T.L. trap automatically varies its direction of throw every time it is re-

[61]

cocked by the puller. This is done by means of ratchets round a circular plate on the top surface of which are several cylindrical knobs of heights ranging from about $\frac{1}{4}$in. to 1in; the action of re-cocking the trap moves it across the round plate beneath it and, according to which of the knobs it bears against, so a pawl clicks into one of the teeth on the circumference, locks the trap, and fixes the direction in which it points. The next time it is cocked the circular plate moves round slightly, the trap bears against a different knob and is set to face a new direction. This brief description should convince you that the automatic trap does change its direction for each throw but it should also prompt you to sit in the traphouse and watch the trap being operated; you may then agree with the experts who reckon that the 'automatic' functioning of the trap is not entirely random in its selection of directions, nor free from human interference: the puller can influence the functioning of the direction-setting mechanism, albeit unintentionally. And this brings us to the difficult trick of 'reading the trap'.

Before shooting begins the trap is set to throw a clay about 50 yards, and its vertical angle is such that the clay will be about 10 feet up at 10 yards from the trap; exact figures are quoted in the Rules but approximate ones will suffice to understand where the clays are likely to go. The trap can also throw its targets at about 45° on either side of a line from the firing marks through the traphouse. An experienced trapshooter, after watching for a while, can 'read' a very nearly regular sequence into the horizontal angles selected by the trap and so he is able to predict where the next clay will go; this gives him an advantage because he can be looking in the right direction, expecting the clay, instead of having to watch centrally, not knowing which line his target is likely to take. See Figure III.

Reading the trap is by no means a certainty and even those shooters who have been at the game for years and years know that they are likely to be wrong five times out of a hundred; and when they are wrong they are definitely 'caught on the wrong foot' because they are looking, aiming, expecting, concentrating in one direction and the target flashes out at quite

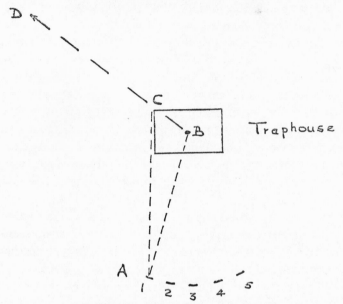

FIG. III. – READING THE TRAP

AB. Normal aim when calling for clay.
AC. Aim when reading the trap, having decided that next clay is going in direction *BD*. The shooter has an advantage in that his gun has already moved part of the way towards where he will make his kill, provided that his reading is correct.

a different angle, which necessitates a quick adjustment of aim and may well result in a miss. Learning to read the trap can only be done by experience and some people find it more difficult than others; the majority are not prepared to make any bets on where the next clay is going and they prefer to

[63]

look away from the trap between shots and then, when it is their turn to shoot again, they expect the target to come out at any angle and so they are not deceived by having concentrated on the wrong one.

You should know about this trap reading business although you may never acquire the experience to do it properly, particularly as the electric trap, which is self-cocking and self-loading is now coming into use.

The automatic trap will probably survive for several years among the smaller clubs but the more expensive electric trap will be used for major competitions; it really is automatic in its random selection of angles and it cannot be read. The release mechanism is also electric, actuated by pressing a button and this speeds up the operation so that when the shooter calls 'Pull!' the puller instantly presses the electric button and the clay is away. The old-fashioned puller, working his big lever like a railwayman in a signal box, can affect the shooter by being slow in his pulling; it may be only a fraction of a second but if it varies it can spoil the rhythm of the shooter who says to himself, all in a matter of a second : 'Now I'm ready; watch that spot; pull; damn! the clay hasn't appeared; oh yes it has; blast! too slow, I missed it.'

The shooter *wants* to think! 'Ready; pull; there it is; fire!' all in one smooth sequence which can be spoilt by a bad puller or even a partisan one. Hence the need for strictly neutral pullers in competitions; in team matches it is usual for each team to take their own pullers with whom the members have become accustomed to shooting. The electric trap means a genuinely unpredictable angle for the clay and instantaneous release as soon as the shooter calls for his bird; he must then be watching centrally ready to swing to either side and he should address the trap itself, which actually is out of sight inside its housing, and not point his gun to one side of the traphouse as he would if he was reading the trap. The slightly low aiming point, below the traphouse roof, makes sure that the barrels will be raised up to the clay when it appears whereas if the gun is pointed over the top of the traphouse a target skimming low out to one side would mean that the barrels have to be lowered slightly and this makes the shot erratic. (Plate 18.)

You can start trapshooting using an ordinary double-barrelled game gun but most serious shooters prefer the single sighting plane, unencumbered by side-by-side barrels, of an over-and-under gun or a single barrel repeater. In game shooting you watch the bird and point your gun at it, the correct fitting and mounting of the gun ensures that it points where your eye is looking, and you do not see the muzzles as accurately focused objects because you are watching your bird; in clay shooting you are often allowed to mount the gun to your shoulder and aim the gun before the target appears. For this reason some guns, as well as having a bead foresight, have a second small bead about half-way along the rib, but the value of this extra bead is an arguable point. It probably has very little value. 30-inch barrels are good for Down-The-Line because long-barrels produce less muzzle blast than short ones, and a fairly heavy gun is an advantage because it is steadier and gives less recoil than a light weapon. The barrels should be about $\frac{1}{2}$-choke and full choke. The novice finds it difficult to get off his shot quickly enough and he may fire at a clay 40 or more yards away so a fair degree of choke is called for, especially as the target is so small. The clay normally reaches its zenith at about 18 yards from the trap, which is 18 +16, 34 yards from the firing mark; for success the shooter must take his shot inside this distance, say at about 30 to 32 yards and to do this he has to be very quick and fire as soon as he sees the clay and his brain registers its

[65]

direction of flight; if he waits until the clay begins to drop the shot becomes more difficult and of course the range is increased to 40 yards or more.

The D.T.L. gun needs a fairly straight stock, certainly not more than the standard $1\frac{1}{2}$ inches drop at the comb. Such a gun will normally throw the centre of its pattern about 16 inches high at 40 yards which is an advantage because:

1. We all have a tendency to shoot low.
2. Nearly all misses, as well as being behind, are also low.
3. There is an inclination to want to see the target, just, at the moment of firing, instead of blotting it out. Therefore a gun which shoots a bit high will still put its shot charge on the target.

Some of the cheaper factory-made guns have too much drop at the comb so if you own one of these you should measure the drop by placing a ruler along the top of the barrel, jutting out over the comb, and measuring the distance between the lower edge of the ruler and the comb. If there is too much drop the comb should be built up, and here again you will do better to consult the expert gunsmith rather than try to stick on some sort of pad yourself.

A special type of stock, called a Monte Carlo, has the comb built up so that it is brought back horizontally along the top, parallel to a prolongation of the sighting plane along the rib; it is then cut away sharply at the heel so that the size of the butt plate bearing against the shoulder remains normal. The horizontal line of the comb is said to keep the eye at the same level if the cheek slides along the stock when swinging the gun to the side; this, however, shows faulty teaching and practice: correct gun mounting puts the butt hard into the shoulder, the cheek glued to the stock and then when you swing you do so with the body, not the arms, and the cheek must not move on the stock. Try it with a gun now; stop reading and get up and fetch your gun; mount it, slightly above the horizontal and pointing in front. Now swing round to the left, rather more than a right-angle, pivoting from the hips and then come back and round to the right. Arms, head, gun, cheek and shoulder should move round as a whole, with no movement of one relative to the other. You should be convinced that the normal man has no need for a Monte Carlo stock, although it may well be that he who does use one gains some sort of erroneously based confidence from it.

Before you shoot a complete round of D.T.L. you must get some experience of what the clays look like over a gun barrel and you must learn how to hit them, starting with the easier ones. We will start at No. 3 firing mark and set the trap to throw clays straight out in front.

Stand with your feet in the position shown in Figure I, mount your gun as described in Chapter 3, lean forward a little, weight on the left foot and right heel clear of the ground. Put your gun muzzle on the unseen trap inside its housing, lock the butt solidly into your shoulder with the comb firmly against your cheek, and call 'Pull!'. The instant you see the clay, swing up the muzzle by straightening up your body from the waist, not by raising the arms from the shoulders, and as the gun blots out your sight of the clay, squeeze the trigger. The target is going straight away from you but it is rising and if you miss it the reason is practically certain to be that you shot too low. Try again; swing up the muzzle quickly and shoot. Do NOT, whatever you do, attempt to follow the target, trying to watch it, trying to take extra care. There is no time to be careful, you must shoot quickly. Have several shots at this easy going-away clay until you are confident that you can break it nine times out of ten. Then move a yard to your left, towards No. 2 station and shoot from there, with the trap still set to throw straight out in front. The flight line of your target is now slightly to the left as well as up so the muzzle of your gun must move leftwards and this movement, only quite slight, should come from your body, not your arms. It is a small pivoting from the hips, and again, as the muzzle passes the clay, so you fire. Try some more shots from this position and if you miss do not fire the second barrel, for that would just be a waste at this stage; you must make yourself kill that clay bird when it is no more than 30-odd yards out, before it has passed the apex of its line of flight.

As you learn to break the clays, move outwards in stages of one yard until you come to No. 1 firing mark. The apparent sideways, to the left, movement of the target increases as you move and this must be taken care of by an increasing amount of pivoting from the body. Do not try to 'lead' the target by any specified distance like a couple of feet, but just concentrate on swinging fast right past the clay and pressing the trigger as you go. Persevere at this drill until you are satisfied that you can hit most of the targets. If you cannot hit them at all something is radically wrong and you will have to go to a professional coach to seek out the trouble. You should certainly persuade an experienced friend to accompany you on these early trial shots to see that you are not making any obvious error, but if you follow carefully the steps outlined here you ought not to have much difficulty in breaking a fair number of clays.

Go back to No. 3 mark and work outwards to No. 5, shooting as before at each stage of one yard so that you become accustomed to the right-handed movement of the clays. Most shooters find the swing to the right a little more awkward than that to the left, but that need not be so if you practise your body pivoting and remember that it is the body that

[68]

moves the gun across and not the arms. Keep that swing going fast and make yourself continue on as you fire; do not falter and check the swing as you pull the trigger.

Now return to No. 3 mark and have the trap set to throw at varying angles. This is something new; you do not know where the clay is going. The slightly quartering shots will be familiar to you, since they present the same target as when you were at No. 1 or 5 firing mark and the trap was throwing straight in front. But suddenly a clay will fly out at quite an oblique angle across your front and you will probably miss it behind. Think about these oblique shots and resolve to whip your body round to get onto them, so quickening the swing, and to push those barrels up with the left arm to take care of the fact that the target is rising, and probably more sharply than it appears to be.

Try the other firing marks again, with the trap varying its angles, and when you are at No. 1 or No. 5 you will have some targets which are travelling nearly directly across your front. They are not quite direct crossers but they are near enough so to be easily missed behind. Do not worry about these shots, and above all do not start thinking of any tales you may have heard about how difficult they are or how much the shooter must lead in front of them. If you have not heard much about the vexed subject of forward allowance, so much the better. Strive to keep that swing going, out and past and beyond the point where you pull the trigger, fire as you pass the clay, swing on and keep your cheek glued to the stock. Many apparently unaccountable misses are due to the shooter raising his head to see the result of his shot before he has completed it. The shot is not completed until you have swung on past the spot where you fired. (Plate 19.)

If you cannot master these crossing shots you are missing behind, and probably below as well. You may then have to

[69]

give a little forward lead to the target, but the amount entirely depends on the reactions of you, the individual shotgunner. The quick shot with fast reflexes really does swing quickly through his bird and fire as he passes it, but some of us cannot attain this standard, perhaps because there is too long a time lag between the brain deciding to fire and the finger operating the trigger. The youngster who has not done much shooting may be inclined to flinch as he takes his shot, particularly if he has an ill-fitting gun, and this will certainly check his swing. It is much better to try to improve your swing until you can hit crossing shots, but if you still fail to connect you must hold on until you have swung the barrels beyond the clay and then fire. If you still miss, open out a little more until you score a hit and keep in your mind a picture of what you saw of the relative positions of the barrels and the clay; the picture is important because you have to remember it for future use when you meet the same conditions again. Remember not to slow down the swing just because you are going out in front of the clay and, once again, do not lift your cheek off the stock until well after you have taken the shot.

When you have learnt something about how to hit clays at all the various angles you can try a real round of Down-The-Line, competing against other shooters. When you start to shoot, from whichever firing mark you are allotted, mount your gun calmly, muzzle on that place on the traphouse which you have been aiming at in practice, shoulder and cheek well onto the stock and make yourself give an extra flash of concentration as you call 'Pull!', and get that shot off quickly. From No. 1 mark an extreme left hand angled target will need all your swing and a bit of lead if you found that necessary when you were practising, and when the trap throws its right-hand bird it will present you with a going-

9.
The basic position for picking up a bird, with the muzzles on it and the eye looking past them at it. Weight leaning forward, forefinger on the trigger guard, thumb pushing forward the safety catch. The line Eye-Muzzle-Bird is indicated.

10.
The eye over the barrels. The eye is visible above the rib but no part of the right cheek shows.

11.
Pivoting from the hips. The shooter's front is toward you, and he has swung through a right angle to his right—

12. —and to his left.

13.
This is bad. He has swung his arms across his body and left his hips behind in their original position. The barrels are canted sideways.

14.
Equally bad to the left, arms across and hips not pivoted. Barrels canted again and cheek raised a little off the comb.

15. Never allow yourself to do this. He is pulling a gun out of the car and the muzzles are pointing straight at him.

16.
It is more important to be a safe shot than a good one. This sign is by the door of the hut on a gun club's shooting grounds, to remind the members.

17. On the firing marks at a Down-The-Line competition. No 1 unloads, No. 2 is shooting. No. 3 loads, Nos. 4 and 5 relax.

18. On the traphouse an "X" has been added to the photograph. This is where the shooter pointed his gun as he called for his target; he has now swung up to shoot it.

19. This automatic user has just taken his shot and the cartridge is being ejected. It seems possible that he might have taken his cheek off the stock a little early.

away shot which will only require blotting out with rising barrels. Remember to place your feet so that your front (12 o'clock in Figure I) is towards the trap; this means that your foot position changes slightly when you move along to No. 2 firing mark because your front has changed due to the lateral displacement. Think of the change in angles of the flight lines, which make the extreme left-hander less of a crossing shot now, while the right-hander has a slight right deflection and the one inside it becomes your going-away shot.

From stand 3 the flow of clays is equally divided between right and left of the centre line, which is now your front as far as your foot position is concerned. Keep your drill the same, cheek on the stock, and pivoting the body from the hips in the required direction.

When you are at stand 4 the main flow of targets is slightly to your right and the small variation in angles as you move along the line must be watched very carefully. It is the small angles that deceive so that the shooter tends to treat them as straight going-away shots when in fact they are not; you must get your gun muzzle out to the front edge of the target and on anything but the straight-in-front clay that means on one side or the other. You have to learn to recognise these angles and to do so in a split second so that the instant you see the clay you can swing your gun on and shoot. Never let yourself dwell in the aim, wondering whether you have judged the angle correctly. That is fatal and will never help you to shoot well; you must get your gun on and fire, and patience, experience and practice will help you to kill 25 straight, provided you start correctly.

No. 5 firing mark is the reverse of No. 1, with the right-hand flight line nearly a direct crosser and the left-hand one the going-away shot. Remember to place your feet so as to face correctly to your front, which is towards the trap.

Perhaps you are taking part in a Down-The-Line competition for the first time, so here are a few points to watch. Even if you have already done some competitive shooting you may have missed some of these details.

1. Avoid going in the first squad, so that you have a chance to watch the behaviour of the clays before your turn to shoot arrives.

2. Have a look from a flank and you will see how much the clays are rising. You will also be able to appreciate where, along the line of flight, the experienced shots are breaking their targets.

3. Notice the direction and effect of the wind; if it is from the front towards the trap it will cause the clays to fly higher than usual and if from behind the firing marks to the trap it will hold the clays down on a flatter trajectory. When the wind is from a flank it will raise those clays thrown into it and lower those going in the same direction. The wind may change during the day and even while you are in the firing line, so watch carefully. Take a look at any flags flying from the Committee tent before you shoot and remember that the stronger the wind the more effect it will have on the clays after they have gone about ten yards or so, which means you must get your shot off even quicker than usual. The more difficult the targets become the faster you must shoot; trying to make sure by following the unusual course of a gale-blown clay is fatal to your success. One of the 'tricks of the trade' concerns the aiming point when the clays are being blown on a higher or lower trajectory than normal: if they are going higher, point a little lower on the traphouse, which will give you more upward swing, the better to

[78]

catch the rising target; if the clays are lower than usual aim at a slightly higher point on the traphouse so that there will be only a small upward movement of the gun onto the clay and this will prevent overshooting.

4. When you go to the firing line start to concentrate on the job at once. Clay shooting is a game and it is fun, but if you want success you must be serious while you are actually performing; a great deal of the art lies in closing your mind to outside influence and sources of interference; do not listen to remarks from other people about 'Good luck, Charlie!—So-and-so has just killed the lot—watch that left bird, it's the difficult one', and so on. Forget all the chatter and go in determined to kill.

5. When you are actually shooting think to yourself that there is only one important target to shoot; that is the next one. Make your mind up that you are going to kill it, and you will.

6. Do not count your shots. The referee will tell you when to start, when to move position and when you have finished.

7. Do not keep your score, and certainly do not pay any attention to how the other competitors are faring. The scorer will be keeping a record and all you have to do is mind your own business, which is to kill that next clay!

8. Ignore the spectators. If you feel a bit alarmed while you are watching proceedings as a spectator, comfort yourself by realising that when you are out in front shooting you will not be able to see the onlookers, for they will all be behind you. All you need look at is the traphouse and everything and everybody behind you, except the referee, is forgotten.

After you have been shooting Down-The-Line for a while you will acquire considerable confidence and feel quite reasonably pleased that you can produce scores of 18 or 20 out of 25, but then there may come a time when you find you are not improving. Always half a dozen clays, or maybe only three or four, elude you. So what do you do?

You should check your equipment and your technique. Make a careful pattern test of your gun and the cartridges you normally use; the percentage of shot in the 30-inch circle at 40 yards may be different from what you expected if you have taken for granted the degree of choke in the barrels. Does the gun fit properly? Borrow a friend's gun and see if it feels more comfortable than your own. Check that eye position above the barrel: when you point the gun at your eye in a mirror you should see the whole eye above the breech and if you can only do this by raising your cheek off its correct, snug position on the comb there is probably too much drop on your gun. That will cause you to shoot low and may account for some of those misses, especially at the longer ranges.

How about your style? Are you really swinging with your body and not your arms? Keeping that cheek on the stock until after the shot? Is your stance correct, not standing stiffly upright, not crouching down but leaning forward into the shot, pivoting from the hips, weight on the left leg? The only really satisfactory way of making certain about these matters is to go to a Shooting School and let the coach see you shooting. He will most likely spot some error in your style of which you are wholly unaware.

Handicapping was mentioned in Chapter 1 when it was explained how, in order to give poorer shots a chance of a prize, classes are introduced based on previous form and on age. A handicap may also be imposed by increasing the distance of the firing point from the trap and, apart from using

[80]

this method during the competition, the judges may decide to adopt it in the 'Shoot-off' when more than one competitor ties for first place. In England this is more likely to happen in small club events rather than in important Championships. As soon as you move back from the standard firing marks, 16 yards from the trap, it becomes even more necessary to shoot quickly; as if you hadn't been trying your hardest to do that already! More lead will be required as the range increases, but apart from that there is no special technique for dealing with these progressively difficult targets, except determination not to panic and to keep to the correct drill.

A shortened version of some of the rules may help the inexperienced: for instance, when you hit a clay you score a kill and this usually means three points if it was with the first shot and two points if a second cartridge was needed. A missed bird is termed 'lost' and it is also lost if you do not fire at it due to your own negligence, such as forgetting to load; if you have a genuine misfire the referee is empowered to allow you another shot. 'No bird' is the term used if the clay is released before the shooter calls for it, or if it breaks in the air as it leaves the trap. You should know that a clay must be seen to be broken to count as a kill, and a pellet through a picked up clay is no evidence that it was 'broken'. You ought also to be aware of the fact that a competitor who lightheartedly shoots at a live pigeon crossing the range will be immediately disqualified! You will be very foolish if you enter for a competition without first obtaining a set of rules and being certain you understand them.

An odd expression you may meet is 'Shooting for Birds only'. This refers to a competitor who abrogates his right to any prizes or awards. It sounds like a curious idea, but sometimes a fairly average shot will decide to enter a high-power competition, which he has no chance of winning, to give himself the experience of shooting with first-class shots. He may also reckon that as he is not really in the contest he need not feel so anxious and tense, and this may very well be so, with the result that he shoots remarkably well, perhaps above his normal form. Thus he gains some invaluable confidence in himself. Sometimes, incidentally, this man finds his score up among the prize-winning ones and he wishes he had entered the competition properly, but if he had done so it is quite likely that his lack of experience would have spoilt his ability to relax physically as well as concentrate on his task, and his score would have been much lower.

The body should never be tense for this will cause jerky movements and a checked swing; the physical relaxation ought to be like that of the racing driver who looks comfortable and unruffled as he swings his car through a bend at 120 m.p.h., completely in control and with a smoothness that makes the whole thing look easy. There is no doubt that shooting for birds only is a help to the ambitious beginner who wants to have a go among the top flighters.

Another odd-sounding term is the 'High Gun'. This refers to the gentleman who beats them all. It is generally used in a team match, probably an International one, and is reserved for the champion of champions who, during the whole meeting, produces a better score than all his rivals.

Down-The-Line shooting is great fun but it is a specialised business. If you want success you have to equip yourself adequately, learn all you can about it and practise as much as possible. Even practice without actually shooting is important so that you train your body to handle the gun with speed and ease. Some critics suggest that this form of shooting is harmful for game shooting, particularly because of the unnatural mounting of the gun to the shoulder before the target appears; it would be much nearer the truth to say that this feature of D.T.L. is a help towards game shooting because correct gun mounting, with the gun in the same place against cheek and shoulder every time, is so important; and the very fact that the clay shooter has time to mount his gun carefully, and to correct matters if it feels wrong, improves his gun mounting and induces in him the habit of getting it right all the time. With perfect gun mounting guaranteed, as a result of plenty of practice at it, the D.T.L. marksman has acquired a most definite advantage in all other types of shotgun shooting and, whether he also shoots driven partridges or goes duck flighting, his training in fast and accurate handling will stand him in good stead.

Naturally the sport is followed by specialists and if you go and watch these experts you may easily form a false impression of how easy it is, especially if you have done some game shooting and so consider that the D.T.L. marksman, by having his gun up at the shoulder before he calls for his target, has an 'unfair' advantage over the difficulties of normal shooting. Such was the impression of a certain young man who had done a good deal of rough shooting and, with the help and encouragement of his father, had developed into quite a fair shot. He thought he would have a go at clay pigeon shooting and soon he achieved modest success at some of the small local clubs; there were three little silver cups on the sideboard to remind the family that the son was a pretty good shot, although Father warned him not to have too grand ideas of his prowess or one day he might take a fall which would be painful.

Well, our young man saw a notice one day giving details of the County Championship shoot. It was to be a 50-bird event and all those who killed 20 out of the first 25 birds would be eligible to shoot the next 25 to decide the Championship. That sounded easy enough and during the days before the shoot he began imagining how fine it would be to be called Champion; and on the day he would have been champion, had the lowest score counted . . .

The automatic trap was being used, the first time the youngster had met it, and naturally everyone was calling for their birds from the 'gun up' position, also strange to him. It was a warm summer day and his gun became too hot to handle as he shot off two barrels at each clay, to make a score of 7, the lowest of all the competitors. Deep was his humiliation when he returned home but his father explained that the set-back would do him good : he felt foolish just then but that did not matter because as far as serious shooting was concerned he was now at the bottom and that is the best place from which to make a start, as long as there is determination to do better. And it certainly was, for the young man then set himself to find out what serious clay shooting was all about and in due course he became County Champion and won many other events besides.

If you are learning to shoot Down-The-Line, do not be in too much of a hurry; follow the sequence described in this chapter, get your stance right, and your mounting and then plug away at the easier shots before you go on to the more difficult ones, and practise on them all before you enter for a competition round.

CHAPTER FIVE

SKEET

THIS unusual name comes from an old Scandinavian word meaning 'to shoot' and it is a development of trap-shooting designed to give a variety of shots simulating those found in the field. As game shooting becomes more expensive and difficult to obtain and the opportunities for rough shooting and wildfowling continuously disappear with the spread of new roads and buildings, so the man who wants to enjoy using his gun is faced with more and more obstacles in finding his sport. It is possible in Great Britain to find inexpensive rough shooting but the townsman has to travel a long way for it, necessitating staying away from home for at least a week-end, or more probably making his shooting trip a part of his annual holiday. By shooting Skeet he can have a lot of fun within easy reach of his home and he can learn to shoot well at clays flying at all sorts of different angles, and this will help him when he comes to substitute the real thing for the artificial target. Only a short distance outside many towns throughout the country there is a Skeet layout belonging to the local gun club.

In Down-The-Line all the clays are going away from the shooter and they are shot at ranges of about 30 to 35 yards, whereas at Skeet many of the targets are crossing shots and the range is less, in the region 20 to 25 yards. Study the lay-out diagram at Figure IV. The shot from the high house at No. 1 stand is similar to that at a bird which has come over the shooter's head from behind; although it is flying straight the apparent line of flight is downward and the gun will therefore have to be moved down to keep ahead of the bird. This is quite different from the technique of raising the gun to blot out the target as when taking a straight forward going-

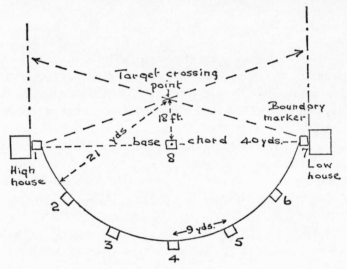

FIG. IV. – SKEET LAYOUT
(Distances are approximate.)

away shot at Down-The-Line. In game shooting it often happens that a bird comes over your head from in front and you have to turn round to shoot it behind; this is a difficult shot and it calls for correct footwork, but it is frequently missed because the gun is not swung down sufficiently. The Skeet shot 'High house, No. 1 stand' will give you practice at the correct gun handling for this situation, made easier by the fact that you can place your feet correctly before the target appears.

Skeet traps are set to throw their clays always along the

[86]

same path and they do not vary the angles as does the auto-matic Down-The-Line trap. The varying types of shot result from the competitors moving round the eight different shoot-ing stations. The high house trap is fired first, throwing its clay from a point about 10 feet from the ground, and then the low house trap releases a clay from a height of $3\frac{1}{2}$ feet. Doubles are also shot at, when both traphouses operate to-gether. The good Skeet shooter kills his birds somewhere near the target crossing point in the centre of the layout, while the inexperienced, slower shot cannot get his gun off until the clay is further along its flight line; but he must not delay too long because the clay has to be broken before it has passed the boundary marker, in line with the traphouse.

The Rules of Skeet are somewhat confusing in that they vary in different localities and so a description of some of the changes is necessary. The differences are generally due to the standard of shooting expected and the consequent need to make the competition reasonably easy or more difficult.

In the early days a Skeet round consisted of 20 birds, and the crossing point for the targets was 8 feet in front of the base chord between the two traphouses, instead of 18 feet as it is now. The shooter, at No. 1 stand alongside the high house, had one cartridge, and took a shot at a clay from the high house, going away from him; he then reloaded and had the incoming bird from the low house. Shots had to be taken from the 'gun down' position, which meant that the butt was below the right elbow and touching the hip. When the Ref-eree saw that the shooter was ready he pressed a button which set off an electric buzzer in the traphouse to tell the trapper to fire off his trap. When the first competitor had taken his two shots the remaining members of the squad had their turns and this was repeated round to stand No. 7. That made 14 clays, so far.

Doubles were then thrown, the shots being taken from stands 6, 4 and 2. The shooter loaded two cartridges and when he was ready the high house trap was released; on the report of his gun as he took his shot the low house trap fired the second clay of the pair. Thus each man had three sets of doubles in turn, making 6 more birds, a total of 20 for the round.

This old-fashioned method of playing the Skeet game is still used sometimes, particularly by small gun clubs where the standard of shooting is not in the expert class. To make it easier, and perhaps as a result of popular demand, the gun down rule is sometimes relaxed and competitors are permitted an 'optional' gun position which means that most of them have their guns up at the shoulder and then call 'Pull', as at Down-The-Line shooting. (Plates 21, 22.)

The Regulations for Skeet produced by the International Shooting Union require a layout as in Figure IV. This places stands 1 and 7 in front of their respective traphouses, and not alongside, and the target crossing point is 18 feet from the base chord which puts the targets further out from the stands and gives more time for Doubles. The extra time does not make Doubles easier, however, because both clays are sent off together instead of the second of the pair being held back until the competitor fires his shot at the first. The I.S.U. Regulations also include stand No. 8, between the two traphouses, where the clays are going nearly over the shooter's head. The gun down position is enforced and when the shooter is ready he calls 'Pull!', but the clay is not released immediately: to make matters a little more difficult an electrical timing device is used so that when the button is pressed to fire the trap an unknown delay of up to three seconds follows before the trap goes off. Singles are shot at stations 1 to 8 and then Doubles at Nos. 1, 2, 6 and 7 in that order, giving 24 birds, and if all these are killed the 25th shot is 'optional' and can be taken at whatever station and from whichever traphouse the shooter chooses. But if all clays are not killed the first shot missed during the round is immediately repeated and the result scored as the 25th 'optional' shot.

Because the I.S.U. rules make Skeet shooting more difficult the proposal to adopt them met opposition and in England the Clay Pigeon Shooting Association passed a resolution in 1960 that 'until further notice' their rules would follow those of the I.S.U. except that :

1. No. 8 station would not be used.
2. Singles would be shot from stations 1 to 7 in that order.
3. Doubles would be shot from stations 7, 6, 4, 2, 1 in that order.
4. Targets would be released instantaneously, on the call 'Pull' for the high house and 'Mark' for the low house.
5. The gun position would be optional.

This modified form of Skeet calls for more skill than the original version, and it requires 25 birds for a round. But some people think that the omission of No. 8 station reduces the appeal of Skeet as a training ground for game shooting. It would also not be easy to convert from the modified form to that of the I.S.U. because the delay of up to three seconds in firing the traps would be confusing when one was used to them going off immediately on calling 'Pull', and shooting from the gun down position is a slight change of technique from shooting with it already at the shoulder when the target is called for, 'gun up,' or 'best use of gun' as it is sometimes called.

[89]

You will see, therefore, that a Skeet competition may follow a local or a National set of rules and so it is important to know just what these are, in detail. The Americans follow closely the I.S.U. rules but in Great Britain the modified form is used even in National competitions; it may be that in the future the C.P.S.A. will alter its rules to conform with the I.S.U. If you attend a small shoot at a local gun club you will probably find the old, easier rules in force as they make the affair more fun for moderate shots who would find the Doubles particularly difficult were both clays to be released at once.

Now for the Skeet gun, what type is best? Because of the comparatively short ranges a big pattern at 20 yards is required and this means an open bored gun. The two shots at No. 8 post are very close and to try to take them with a fully-choked barrel would need some very straight shooting indeed. Improved cylinder in both barrels is a suitable degree of choke for Skeet, but this combination is unusual except in a gun made specially for the job. A game gun or one made for D.T.L. will inevitably have a greater degree of choke in one barrel than the other, so here we come again to that expensive, but eminently satisfactory, solution of having a gun with two sets of barrels: one set is perhaps half and full choke and the other is improved cylinder in both barrels. If you have a single barrelled automatic you are all right if it is open bored but all wrong if it has a full choke, as many of them do. If you can learn to shoot with an automatic, or a pump gun, this will be a much cheaper way of equipping yourself for clay shooting than going in for the gunmaker's delight of ordering two guns or one with two sets of barrels. The single barrel with variable choke attachment can see you through the different types of clay shooting competitions but any type of repeating shotgun is definitely more difficult to manage than a double-barrelled weapon, until you have had a good deal of practice. In the United States the repeater, in one form or another, is very popular and if you attend clay shoots in England you will often find Americans competing and using one of these guns with considerable success. But remember that they have been brought up to use such a shotgun and so have plenty of experience with it. If you can afford two barrels buy them, and if you already own a double-barrelled gun use it for Skeet and, although you will be handicapped if one barrel has a fair degree of choke, do not let that worry you until you decide to take the game seriously enough to expect to win prizes at major events. Then you will have to equip yourself with something more suitable. (Plate 20.)

As always, the final choice of a gun has to be a compromise between conflicting requirements, but a few general points should be born in mind. Unless you are small and not very strong ultra-short barrels are not recommended; 25 or 26-inch barrels can be too light and whippy for the average man to hold steady even though, at Skeet, his target is close and therefore has an apparent speed necessitating some smart gun handling. 28-inch is a good standard but again, as described in Chapter 2, a 30-inch barrel for a strong man and a reasonably heavy gun, about 7 lbs., helps steadiness and a good, unchecked swing . A small, lightly-built man may choose a gun specially made for Skeet and weighing only about 6 to $6\frac{1}{2}$ lbs., arguing that to shoot a round is an energetic performance and can be tiring if a heavy gun is used, but the average physique is better suited with something a little heavier. It is all very well to think that at Skeet Doubles you have to move your gun very quickly from the first clay to the second but it is no good doing so unless the impetus of the gun in your hands is sufficient to keep that swing going

[91]

on the first target until you have hit it, before you change direction onto the second one. Some Skeet shooters use guns of 7½ to 8 lbs. but you certainly would not be advised to get such a heavy gun if you intend to use it for game shooting as well, because the extra pound or so becomes very noticeable after you have been carrying it around for a few hours. In any case, many of these guns are repeaters which, by their nature, have to be heavy.

There is still much to be said in favour of the side-by-side gun for Skeet. The argument in favour of the narrow sighting plane of the prominent rib on the single barrel or over-and-under is more applicable to Down-The-Line. Although over-and-unders are sometimes used in the field it is often accepted, at any rate in England, that a pair of side-by-side barrels are most suitable for game shooting and hence also for Skeet because:

1. Any repeating single barrel must be subject to muzzle disturbance while the ejecting and reloading process is occurring.
2. Multi-shot single-barrelled weapons are nearly always comparatively heavy and badly balanced.
3. The width of two barrels side-by-side, as compared with the narrowness of the raised rib of a trapshooting gun, provides a line, scarcely consciously seen, which assists in keeping the sideways movement of the muzzles parallel to the line of flight of the target. This is mostly applicable on crossing shots, when there is also less tendency to cant side-by-side barrels.

The English Skeet Championship was won in 1968 by E. Grantham, using a side-by-side gun.

From guns to cartridges, and popular sizes are 7, 8 and 9, in fact I.S.U. Regulations allow only these sizes. There are no

20.
A repeater at the moment of shooting a Skeet clay. The ejected cartridge is visible by the breech and the shooter's cheek is pressed well onto the comb.

21. The shot has been taken. This is a good stance with a firm left leg. Note that the waiting competitors have their guns open. The referee is holding a presser switch connected by wire to an electric buzzer in the traphouse.

22. No. 2 mark, taking the low house bird. Note the loose left hand hold favoured by some shooters who correctly regard the left hand as the one that directs the gun onto the target, while the right is the one which grips firmly. Incidentally, the traphouse has some pellet marks on its side!

23.
This Skeet shooter looks over his gun muzzles at the spot where he is going to pick up his target.

24.
He mounts his gun, swings right and shoots. Note the good stance and cheek tightly on the comb. If "gun up" was permitted this would be a good example of the correct position before calling for the target.

25.
After his first shot at Skeet doubles the butt should be slightly lowered like this while the shooter picks up the line of the second clay over the muzzles.

Page 95

26. A bad position from which to call for the target because the butt must be raised considerably when the gun is mounted, and the muzzles will have to be lowered, all of which wastes time.

27. Another bad position, weight back on right leg and barrels too low. The shooter has no idea of the theory of keeping the muzzles between his eye and his target.

28.   At No. 8 stand high house he is ready to shoot, watching intently
for the clay to appear.

long-range shots at Skeet and so if you want the best pattern you may well decide to use No. 9 shot. But remember that individual guns often give better patterns with one size of shot than with another, so that if you are taking things really seriously you ought to test the pattern of your gun with different shot sizes and at a measured range, in this case 25 yards. And pattern testing means firing several cartridges and counting the number of pellets in the 30-inch circle. Pending such careful testing you would be advised to use $1\frac{1}{8}$-oz. of shot, size 8.

Before shooting a round of Skeet it is advisable to have some practice shots at each of the stands. Remember the importance of body control and that the movement of the gun barrels comes from a pivoting at the hips and is not induced merely by waving the arms across the body. Skeet targets always follow the same path and you know that path beforehand, or at least you will do as you gain experience. From any specific shooting stand the body and gun movement is the same for every clay that leaves the high house, and similarly a different movement will be repeated at each clay from the low house. Practice will therefore accustom the body to following a definite line at each stand and once you can find this the shooting becomes comparatively easy, although it appears difficult in the early stages. Stance is important, as always, and the feet should be fairly close together with the shooter's front, 12 o'clock in Figure I, towards mid-field, the target crossing point.

Forward allowance is necessary for all crossing shots, and there are plenty of these at Skeet. Theoretically the angular displacement of the gun ahead of the target is the same at long range, 40 yards, as it is at a close range of 20 yards but in practice the linear amount the shooter must lead his target, the 'picture' he keeps in his mind, described in

Chapter 4, has to be increased at long ranges because the apparent speed of the target is less. For close range Skeet shots you do not need to give much lead but you must give some and the speed of your swing, unchecked as you fire, will be increased by the very fact that the target is so close and you have to move fast to catch it.

Now let us go to No. 7 shooting mark and try the outgoing clay from the low house. Stand with the target crossing point as your front, sway forward a little onto your left leg, right heel just clear of the ground and look about 10 or 12 feet out from the traphouse where you expect to see the clay. If the rules allow gun up this is where your gun will be aiming, if gun down is the rule you should look over the end of the barrels at this point in the air, being careful not to focus your eyes in a fixed stare on some object a long way off in the background. Call for your clay and you will see it going out and up very nearly straight away from you; lift the gun by raising your body from the hips, just as you did when you started Down-The-Line from No. 3 firing mark, blot out the target with the muzzles and shoot, but keep the gun moving up and hold your cheek on the stock a little longer than you think necessary. If you stop the gun and raise your head to see the effect of your shot it is practically certain that all you will see will be the clay sailing on out beyond the boundary marker. It is so important, this instruction to hang onto the swing and hug the cheek against the stock that it has to be repeated even if the repetition becomes somewhat tedious. If, as a learner, you can make yourself start correctly you will be saved a great deal of trouble correcting faults later and you will start making good scores much sooner. If you have done quite a bit of shooting it is a good idea to make sure you are keeping cheek to stock by exaggerating the time you hold it there, by ordering yourself

'Cheek!', immediately after you fire and holding your cheek on for a second before you lower the gun. You will then probably find that you hit targets that you used to miss.

You should not have much difficulty in killing this bird from No. 7 stand, and it will have helped you to become accustomed to the idea of not looking at the exit hole of the traphouse, called the chute, but at a point in front of it, and of shooting your target in midfield.

Now try No. 6 stand, still from the low house, and you will find a slight sideways, to the left, angle is the clay's line of flight. Keep that swing going and shoot as the muzzles pass the target a little above it. A rising partridge or pheasant presents a similar quartering shot and a good point to re-member in such circumstances is to try to shoot above the bird's neck, for it is all too easy to miss below on any rising target.

The next outgoer to try is No. 1 from the high house. Look out in front of the chute about 12 to 15 feet, either past the end of your gun barrels or along the rib, according to whether you are shooting gun down or gun up. It is no good trying to watch the clay coming out of the traphouse because it is travelling too fast, you must watch that point in space where you expect to see the target and then immediately mount the gun when it appears. The muzzles should follow down the apparent course of the clay, as you bend forward from the waist, and your forward allowance is below it, so that you can still see it at the moment of firing; if it dis-appears behind the barrels it is a lost bird, you have missed. This is just the opposite to 'blotting out' on a straight-away rising target. It is a more difficult shot than your first one, from No. 7 stand, which appeared at about eye level but you should practise it until you are confident you can score a kill most times, remembering not to bring the gun ahead of the target merely by pulling down with your left arm. That would produce a jerk not a swing, and it would also tend to disturb the important position of your cheek on the stock and your eye just above the rib. Once your gun is mounted, on any shot, you ought to be able to move it around through rather more than a right angle, horizontally to either side and vertically over your head, by body movement from the hips and without altering your stance, with the weight on your left foot. A school of thought exists which maintains that the gun should be raised to the target at No. 1 high house, because the clay itself is rising, but this is a complicated way of thinking which makes the problem more difficult instead of easier. It also is at variance with the principle that the line of any moving target should be picked up with the gun muzzles and followed precisely until and beyond the moment of firing; and the apparent path of the clay from No. 1 stand is downward, so therefore the barrels must move down.

Stand 2, high tower, gives a target requiring a little sideways lead as well as downward, in the direction of 5 o'clock on an imaginary clock face whose centre is the clay. Here the hips bend forward slightly to bring the barrels down and they pivot to the right to swing in front of the target. Look at a point about 12 feet out from the traphouse.

You should try some incomers next, starting from No. 7 stand high house, and facing again to mid-field, which is where you are going to kill your bird. It is approaching you, rising and going slightly to your right. As you are now 40 yards from the traphouse you ought to be able to see the clay a bit earlier on its flight, and as this is nearly towards you the place to look is not quite at the chute but about a couple of feet to the right of it and about one foot higher. Swing up and right and practise until you get the feel of the 'groove' in which your body moves for this shot; the swing and small lead is similar to stand 2, which you have just left, only the vertical movement is now up when previously it was downward.

At stand 6 you must open out your picture a little more to keep in front of the target, which is coming from the high house. Look a little further to the right of the traphouse chute, about four feet, having first faced your front, midfield, and then pivoted to the left. If you have difficulty with this shot go back to No. 7 and work out gradually a yard at a time so that you become accustomed to the increasing angle of the flight line; stop when you miss and shoot again until you hit, and continue until you are at stand 6. This method is often more helpful than firing away at a new stand, missing the clays and so losing that confidence which is so necessary for successful shooting.

Back to No. 1 stand and we will try the incomer from the low house which requires the same lead as the shot you have just mastered, only this time to the left so you should soon be able to get the correct picture of the muzzles passing the target. Again you are 40 yards from the traphouse so you can look fairly close to the chute, about two feet out from it. Remember that you do not want to kill this bird when it is close to you, nearly opposite the traphouse, but out there at the target crossing point. If you delay your shot you will have to swing much faster and give more forward allowance and you will turn an easy shot into a difficult one.

For No. 2 low house the lead increases and again you may find it helpful to work out gradually from stand 1 to 2, taking shots every yard or so. You should pick up the clay about four feet out from the chute.

Now you should try stands 7, 6, 1 and 2, the ones at which you have been practising, and have a bird from each house, not as doubles but one after the other, taking the bird from the nearer house first because that is the normal way of shooting doubles, which you will be doing a little later. Try to remember how you took these shots previously; get your feet settled comfortably, pivot so that your eye and gun are pointing at the place in front of the chute where you know you can expect to see the clay, and call up in your mind the appropriate picture of the amount of lead each target requires.

The middle shooting stations, numbers 3, 4 and 5 offer quartering shots increasing to full crossing birds and we will start at No. 5 low house. As you approach the centre line the upward angle of the clay's line of flight becomes less acute but you must still watch it carefully and swing the gun right along the true path of the target from the moment you see it until you swing ahead and pull the trigger. Take your stance towards mid-field, pivot to the right and watch for the clay about ten feet out from the chute. You will need a little more lead than at No. 6 stand and when you have killed some birds you can move round a few yards towards No. 4 stand. As you move along increase your lead until, when you reach No. 3 stand you will be taking a direct crossing shot, provided you break the clay at the target crossing point. No one but you can decide how much lead is required and in any case this will depend on the speed of your swing. To start with you ought to concentrate on hitting the targets at the crossing point and this will allow you to try for a constant amount of lead at each stand. If you wait until after the crossing point the angle of the line of flight will change and so will the necessary amount of lead. If, with experience, you can catch the target before mid-field the angle and lead will again change. It would be worth your while to study Figure IV and lay a ruler along the flight line from one of the traphouses. Then place a short pencil with one end on, say, No. 3 stand and running through the crossing point. If you then hold one end of the pencil over No. 3 stand and move the other end along the ruler you will see how the angle alters between pencil (line of flight of shot) and ruler (line of flight of clay), according to whether the gun was fired before or after reaching the crossing point.

Having mastered these crossers from No. 3 stand low house, have the clays thrown from the high house when, from where you are at No. 3, the lead required will be more than it was at No. 2 but about the same as No. 5 low house which you were learning a short while ago. Watch for your target about ten to twelve feet out from the traphouse, body and gun pivoted to the left, and swing smoothly and surely through the clay. Again, move round through stand 4 and 5, increasing the lead as you go until you have defeated that crossing shot to the right which often is, although it ought not to be, a more difficult task than the crosser to the left. (Plates 23, 24, 26, 27.)

No. 8 stand offers two nearly overhead shots which are also low and appear to be moving very fast indeed. If you go straight to this stand and try to shoot you will probably be quite bewildered by the speed of the clays and you will easily fall into the bad habit of taking futile snap shots at them.

To gain confidence, start a few yards in front of No. 7 stand facing through No. 8 position, and take the high house targets, watching about three feet to the right of the chute. Swing up through the clay the instant you see it and make every effort to kill it before it reaches the crossing point. Move in by stages of a couple of yards towards No. 8 stand. If, as you approach No. 8 you find you miss many birds do not despair, the detailed technique of shooting there will be described presently. Go to No. 1 stand and try some of the low house clays, again moving in towards No. 8; when you miss, stay where you are and call for another target until you break it. As you move in towards the centre you are encountering progessively more difficult targets but you should be breaking a fair number of them and learning to quicken up your swing as you approach the line of flight.

Now we will shoot from No. 8 stand, taking the high house first. It is only 20 yards away and you are going to kill that bird when it is about 15 yards out from the trap. Take up your normal stance with your front 15 yards along the flight line, that is rather more than 5 yards from the crossing point. Mount the gun and aim at the spot where the kill is to be and then pivot left until the gun points about two feet to the right of the chute. Lower your right hand so that the butt comes down to your hip but keep the muzzles where they were with your eye looking past them. Do not move your head one inch. You are now ready to call for the target, from the gun down position which will be obligatory if you are shooting to rules which include No. 8 stand in the Skeet round. (Plate 28.)

The instant the bird appears your gun muzzles will be on it, and as you raise the butt to your shoulder you pivot from the waist to swing the gun right and up, eye and muzzle never leaving the target. Do not drop your head and when you feel your cheek on the stock and the butt into your shoulder, press the trigger. Keep leaning forward, do not sway back onto the right leg, and carry the swing through to a nearly vertical position. (Plate 29.) The quicker you can take this shot the easier it is; at 15 yards the angular displacement of the clay is not very much and you need not worry about forward allowance because the fast, unchecked swing of the gun will take care of that. If you delay, however, the target becomes a very fast crossing shot for which you would have to pivot round through a right angle; the gun would have to be swung extremely quickly and it would be difficult to open out to the necessary lead in the split-second time available. Therefore it is most important to sight the clay over the muzzles as soon as possible, to hold it there and to fire as soon as the gun is properly mounted.

When you take the low house target at No. 8 stand you will find that it starts lower but climbs to the same height as the one from the high house. This extra rate of climb does not appreciably affect the nature of the shot. Your stance should be the same, pointing towards that spot 15 yards along the flight line, and you then mount the gun, pivot right and down until you are aiming about two feet to the left of and a foot above the chute; lower the butt, keeping eye and muzzles in line and you are ready.

Be especially careful at No. 8 stand not to raise the head, watching the rising clay, taking the cheek off the comb and so leaving the barrels trailing behind the target. Do not try to jerk the swing but keep it smooth and as you become familiar with shooting from No. 8 you will find you have more time to kill your bird than you thought. If you have real difficulty move out towards No. 1 or 7 stand, opposite to whichever traphouse you are facing, and gather some more confidence by taking the easier shots which give you more time to follow them.

We still have to practise the doubles, shot at stations 1, 2, 6 and 7 by I.S.U. rules and 7, 6, 4, 2 and 1 by C.P.S.A. rules. Whatever the order of shooting you have experienced these shots as singles so all you have to learn is the technique required to deal with two clays in the air at once. Initially, it would be a good idea to have the second clay thrown as you fire at the first, as is still done in the smaller competitions, because this gives more time to deal with number two of the pair.

The outgoing clay, that is the one from the trap nearer to you, is normally shot first. Take your stance towards the crossing point and after your first shot lower the butt slightly off your shoulder and replace it immediately the muzzles are on the line of the second target. (Plate 25). This will help to pick up the second clay more smoothly than if you tried to keep the stock up all the time, and if the butt had been slightly jerked out of place by the first shot it will be correctly positioned again for the second. Even if the rules allow a gun up position for the first shot it is wrong and a definite handicap to try to hold the gun at the shoulder afterwards, and to push the barrels back in the opposite direction without first removing the butt from the shoulder. After the first shot do not be in too much of a hurry to get onto the second clay, otherwise your swing on the first one will be checked and you will miss it. On the other hand you cannot afford the time to pause and admire the shattering effect of your first barrel before you turn your attention to the next target.

As your skill improves you will be able to kill the first bird just before it reaches the crossing point, and then it will be advantageous if your initial stance faces that killing spot because it will also be the line to your killing place for the second target, which of course will have had time to travel a little beyond the mid-field crossing point. This slight change in the direction of your stance will reduce the amount of body pivoting required for the two shots.

Sometimes Skeet learners find they do better at doubles than they expected, and perhaps better than they do at singles. This is because they have had to speed up their swing and so have stopped missing behind. Good shots are always fast but of course merely being fast does not make a good shot; he must also train his body movements to be smooth and steady, co-ordinated with his eye on the target.

To summarise this method of learning the various shots at Skeet, we did our practising in the following order:

No. 7 stand low house.
,, 6 ,, ,, ,,
,, I ,, high ,,
,, 2 ,, ,, ,,
,, 7 ,, ,, ,,
,, 6 ,, ,, ,,

,, I ,, low ,,
,, 2 ,, ,, ,,

,, 7 ,, both houses in turn.
,, 6 ,, ,, ,, ,, ,,
,, I ,, ,, ,, ,, ,,
,, 2 ,, ,, ,, ,, ,,

,, 5 ,, low house
,, 4 ,, ,, ,,
,, 3 ,, ,, ,,

,, 3 stand high house.
,, 4 ,, ,, ,,
,, 5 ,, ,, ,,
,, 8 ,, ,, ,,
,, 8 ,, low ,,

Doubles.

When you try your first competition round of Skeet, or when you watch one as a spectator, you will see some odd styles of shooting most of which are not to be recommended. Some shooters crouch in an awkward-looking posture and others bend their left knee as they prepare for the shot. This is done with the idea of winding up the body, having faced the position where the clay is to be hit, as the shooter turns towards the traphouse watching for the clay to appear; he thinks he can then unwind his twisted position as he follows the flight of the target. But the habit does not make for steady shooting and it is better to keep the left leg firmly braced and pivot from the hips, pushing forward from the toes of the right foot; the gun will then follow a much steadier arc across the sky, because any form of crouch tends to make the barrels wobble unsteadily as they are swung. (Plates 30, 31, 32.)

If the left knee is bent the amount of bend will vary; try pointing your gun at a stationary mark and then quickly bend the left knee, and see if you are still on target. When swinging one cannot maintain a constant degree of knee bend but it is possible to stand firmly on a straight left leg and follow exactly along the flight line of the target. The more complicated anything, including shooting, is made the more difficult it becomes and the greater is the likelihood that something will go wrong. Therefore we try to avoid crouching, winding up and unwinding, moving the feet between shots and any variation of the elementary theory of adopting a normal stance towards the point where the clay is to be hit, pivoting to where it will be picked up over the gun barrels, and thus being perfectly balanced for the shot. (Plate 33.)

It is also possible that you may watch someone shooting a clay going to his right and you notice that he has his right leg forward in front of his left. This is quite wrong; it tends to check the swing, and to make the barrels cant sideways and the shot to go low; it is also completely at variance with the basic teaching of gun mounting by which you can, from the normal stance, pivot round to either side without ever altering the position of eye over muzzle and cheek on stock, and without dropping the weight back onto the right leg. (Plate 34.)

As you start your first round of Skeet, remember at No. 1 stand not to look back impatiently at the traphouse, wondering when the clay will appear. Always look at that spot out in front where you are going to pick up the target. Try to relax your eyes and not stare fixedly; look beyond the gun muzzles and open your eyes wide just before you call for the target.

You will notice many shooters having a slow motion practice swing before they take their shot: they point the gun towards the traphouse, swing out to where they expect to make their shot and then swing back again; then they call for the target. If this is allowed, and sometimes it is not, it may be a good idea to help to put the body in the required 'groove', but the experienced shot knows that swinging on an imaginary line cannot really be of much advantage. I.S.U. Regulation permit the gun to be held in the aiming position for a few seconds, but only at stations 1 and 8: at No. 1 because the competitor may reasonably wish to refresh his memory of the feel of gun mounting for the first shot of the round, and at No. 8 because it is unusual and something of a trick shot. At other stands it is not necessary, since one ought to be able to select the correct stance without the doubtful help of this ungainly procedure.

You will also see people blowing into the breech of their guns after each shot so that the smoke left in the barrel is pushed out through the muzzle. This habit is based on the idea that the smoke might issue slowly out during the next shot and that it could catch the shooter's eye and disturb his aim. Such a circumstance is most unlikely to happen and 'blowing down the spout' is really just a harmless habit, possibly begun as a mild form of affectation. Serious exponents of the practice might, however, claim that the action helps in a small way to keep the barrels cool.

If there is a wind blowing over the Skeet layout it need not deter you; it might speed up some of the clays and slow down others, but at the close range where you are going to kill them they will be dead birds before the effect of the wind can make much noticeable difference to your technique. A point to remember about a really strong wind, however, is that it can push you off balance as you take your shot and therefore you should brace yourself in these circumstances to withstand the force of the wind. It may be that a slightly wider stance than usual will be a help; it is certain that a straight left leg rather than any form of bending will keep you on a firmer footing. And this goes for any form of shooting.

You should try to call up in your mind the flight lines of the clays from every stand, and think about them when you are away from the shooting ground. Go through each shot mentally and remember your picture at the moment of firing, and how the forward allowance looked. You may be somewhat confused by your first complete round but persevere at getting the mental image of each shot correct. Watch others shooting and think about the varying angles of the clays as you go home. If you find that you do not improve after reaching a certain standard you will have to keep practising at your weak shots, but remember that if you can score 15 out of 25 you must be able to shoot, and practice and self criticism will soon improve your scores. When you are practising, analyse what happened when you missed. Is the stance correct to allow full body swing? Was the gun locked into your shoulder and are you positive you did not raise your head? Do not overdo the shooting practice so that you become tired and dispirited, but at the same time do put in some dry practice and exercises, as described in Chapter 9. Practising gun mounting with a fixed object as an aiming point is well worth while but there is not much advantage in practising swinging without having some specific line to follow, be it the flight of a starling or rook or the line of a telephone wire. To swing along an imaginary line serves little purpose but if you swing your gun along any visible line you can see if the barrels waver off it during gun mounting or afterwards, and you may be surprised to find how easy it is to become a little unbalanced and so fail to hold steadily on the line. It should convince you of the importance of a good stance and of how a bent left knee can upset your balance.

To improve your Skeet shooting you will have to use a good many cartridges and clays but you can also help yourself by doing exercises. But you must *do* them and not only read about them in a book.

As a tailpiece in less serious vein, here is a story of the final round at a gun club's Skeet competition. It was being conducted in the old-fashioned way and doubles were being shot at stands 6, 4 and 2. A cheerful company were enjoying themselves and pulling each other's legs in a manner never seen at serious 'must-concentrate-all-the-time' events. Two of the shooters were tying for first place and both killed their doubles from stand 6. As they moved to stand 4 one of them pulled out his snuff box and took a pinch. His opponent, thinking it must be something helpful to shooting, asked, 'What's that?', and he replied 'Oh, I always take it, it clears your eyes'.

'Can I have some?' asked the other fellow.

'Of course, help yourself!'

And number 2 took a good pinch and sniffed it up his nostrils.

Number 1 then killed his pair at stand 4 and his friend moved up for his shot. As the first bird appeared he sneezed hugely, the second bird was released and it too was greeted by an enormous sneeze; both birds were 'lost'. That fixed the final placing and only then did number 1 admit that he had only pretended to take snuff, so that wild and vehement indeed were the curses poured upon him by his rival. But everyone enjoyed the joke and the victim was as cheerful as the rest at the party afterwards for, after all, Skeet shooting is primarily meant to be enjoyed and to provide fun for those who participate.

29. A quick swing up, weight still forward and he fires. The gun will swing on to the vertical before he takes his cheek off the comb and he will not drop his weight back onto the right leg.

30. Crouching looks awkward but it is often seen. From this position he is considerably handicapped in trying to maintain a level swing without the barrels waving up and down.

31.
The Skeet shooter has pointed his gun to the left, where he hopes to kill his bird, and then wound up his body to the right where he expects to see the clay appear. He has bent his left knee and twisted his body round: not recommended.

32.
Now he has unwound back to the left, unsteadily. His feet are too far apart and his cheek is raised off the stock.

33.
He is shooting Skeet under local rules permitting "gun up." For a bird from the low house (out of the picture to the right) he aims his gun along the expected flight line and incorrectly bends his left leg, which action is supposed to help him to swing to his left for the shot; in fact, it makes his stance unbalanced, which may cause the gun to waver off the line.

34.
The stance was wrong in the initial preparation for the shot. The right foot is in front, he is swinging to his right and while actually taking the shot his body is strained, the swing has been checked and the barrels are canted.

Page 118

CHAPTER SIX

OLYMPIC TRENCH

AT International Clay Shooting Championship meetings
Skeet is often included but Down-The-Line has generally be-
come superseded by what is called '15 trap Olympic Trench'.
At the Grand Prix of Great Britain or the Coupe Des
Nations, the European Championships or the Olympic
Games you will find Olympic Trench being shot.

The targets are faster than at Down-The-Line and the
shooting is more difficult. The term 'trench' is used because
the traps are installed below ground in a trench, a substan-
tial affair usually made of concrete and about 72 feet long;
it has a roof, is closed at the back and sides but has a gap in
front 20 inches high above the trap carriers. The traps are
firmly set in concrete and there is plenty of room behind for
the trappers to walk along to attend to them, and for storage
of clays. The traps, which have very strong springs, are fixed
in five batches of three and all are set at the start of a competition to fire in different directions and at varying elevations. In each of the groups of three, which are about 5 yards
apart, the centre trap fires more or less to the front, the left-
hand one to its right and the right-hand one to its left; this
is arranged so that in whatever direction the clay goes it
first appears to the shooter in approximately the same place,
very soon after leaving the trap and close, to the ground.
See Figure V, and Plates 35, 36, 37, 38.

At 10 yards from the trap the clay may be anything from about a foot off the ground to 13 feet and it may go anywhere within about 45° of the line from the shooter to the trap. The minimum range at the best elevation is 77 yards, which means that the initial speed of the clay is indeed high, remembering that a D.T.L. clay is thrown only 55 yards. The

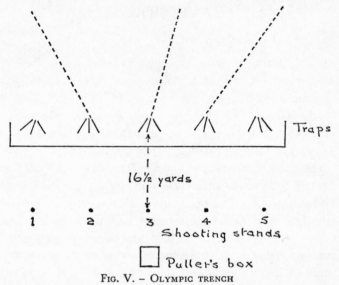

FIG. V. – OLYMPIC TRENCH

Each group of three traps faces more or less Left, Right and Centre, but none are at the same angle. Target lines of flight are indicated for: the right hand trap opposite No. 2 stand; the centre trap opposite No. 3 stand; the left hand trap opposite No. 4 stand.

'puller' is usually in a small raised hut behind the shooting line and he releases the traps mechanically, an electrical circuit being the best system, modern ones having a numbered press button for each trap; in order to produce a random selection of which trap in any group of three is released, the operator is equipped with cards on which are printed numbers previously decided upon by working out a mathematical permutation of all the trap numbers 1 to 15 and the stand numbers 1 to 5; the operator presses the numbered trap buttons in the order in which he sees corresponding numbers on his card. As each shooter calls for his target he knows it will appear from one of the group of three traps in front of him, but neither he nor anyone else outside the operator's box knows which one it will be. An even newer type of release mechanism involving only one button for each set of three traps, one of which is selected at random by an electrical device. Reading the trap is impossible not, as with the automatic electric trap in Down-The-Line, because the trap is varying the angles, but because of the unknown selection of which fixed trap will be fired next. On the latest layouts, a system of 'sonic release' is used: the shooter's call of 'Pull' releases the target without the need for any buttons to be pressed.

Five shooters take up their positions at the firing marks, with a sixth standing behind No. 1, who fires first. The line is straight and not on an arc as with Down-The-Line. No. 1 prepares for his shot (the gun up position is permissible), calls 'Pull' and takes his clay, firing both barrels if he so wishes. He then prepares to move towards No. 2 firing mark after the shooter there has had his shot, and the sixth man moves up to No. 1 mark. Each man in the line has one target in turn, moving on immediately afterwards to the next mark, and by having six men in the squad there is no delay while the shooter at No. 5 walks round to No. 1 position. You will note that only one clay is taken at a time at each mark, and not five as at Down-The-Line. (Plate 39.)

Although the horizontal angles at which a Down-The-Line trap releases its clays are varied, the vertical angle at which it fires remains constant, whereas at Olympic Trench each of the fifteen traps is set at a different elevation as well as a different horizontal angle, so adding to the difficulty of the sport. The referee normally stands behind the shooter and the I.S.U. Regulations require him to give a 'distinct signal' for every missed target; often he does this by squeezing the rubber bulb of a small hooter whenever he sees a miss, and he is helped in any doubtful decisions by two assistants who stand one at each end of the line. (Plate 40). Scoring is 'kills to count', which means that a point is awarded whether the clay is broken with the first or the second barrel. Many competitors fire both barrels quickly at every target, just to make sure in case there is any doubt about the success of the first shot. In the big competitions with a very high standard of shooting one kill may make all the difference in placing in the final results. At an important shoot a few years ago a comparative newcomer to the sport asked one of the competitors why he always fired both barrels when he was so good a shot that, almost without exception, he broke the clay at the first attempt. The expert explained, with a great deal of seriousness, that he just had to fire both barrels because if he only fired one it became very hot and so, with a cold barrel next to it, the gun would become warped; this would obviously cause the gun to shoot crookedly, 'round a corner' so to speak. 'Therefore,' said this benefactor to any young shot who cared to ask his advice, 'I shoot off both barrels to keep the gun evenly warm'. The learner digested this information, and afterwards was never quite certain how much his leg had been pulled and how much his informant really believed in the strange theory. Many shooting men do have peculiar ideas about at least one of the several complexities of their sport but, if the reasons for their subsequent actions are a trifle illogical, no harm is done provided that the results are satisfactory. Firing both barrels at a Trench clay costs more in cartridges but it might save an important lost bird; hence its popularity with the really serious performers. Another genuine reason given by some shooters for always firing both barrels is that it keeps the trigger-finger accustomed to taking the second shot if it really should be needed; they sometimes fire at the pieces of target broken by the first shot.

A round is 25 birds but results are decided on 100, or sometimes 200 spread over two or more days. The traps are $16\frac{1}{2}$ yards (15 metres) in front of the shooting marks and the shortest range at which a clay is likely to be broken is about 37 yards, while a second barrel may be fired at a target as much as 50 yards out, and therefore a tightly bored gun is needed. $\frac{3}{4}$-choke for one barrel and full choke for the other may be regarded as standard and, as with Down-The-Line, a fairly heavy gun is usually preferred. There are not many Olympic Trench layouts in the United Kingdom but if you have a chance to shoot on one you should certainly take it, if only for experience and to see how good shots at Down-The-Line can come to grief when they try Trench and find their accustomed '25 straight' turned into a score of about 17. If your gun has $2\frac{1}{2}$-inch chambers and is proofed for $1\frac{1}{8}$-oz. of shot you can still try Trench shooting without being seriously handicapped, but it is true that many of the experts prefer a bigger gun with $2\frac{3}{4}$-inch chambers and capable of taking the larger cartridge containing $1\frac{1}{4}$-oz. of shot. You must *not*, however, put a $2\frac{3}{4}$-inch cartridge in your smaller gun, even if the crimped closure allows the cartridge to fit into the chambers. This dangerous situation can arise because, since the introduction of crimp closure, the actual length of the loaded $2\frac{3}{4}$-inch cartridge has been reduced, and is now the same as that of the $2\frac{1}{2}$-inch crimped cartridge, i.e. $2\frac{3}{8}$-inch; only the empty case is $2\frac{3}{4}$-inch long. The result of this is that modern $2\frac{3}{4}$-inch crimped cartridges will fit into $2\frac{1}{2}$-inch chambered guns, but if they are fired, the gun is subjected to a higher pressure than that for which it was intended and it may be strained. Most British cartridges are described nowadays by the length of gun chamber for which they are intended, and neither the length of the empty case, nor the loaded case can be taken as a guide.

To add to the confusion but in amplification of the preceding sentences, it should be noted that some trapshooting $2\frac{3}{4}$-inch cartridges are sold loaded so as to be safe in standard $2\frac{1}{2}$-inch chambered guns. The potentially dangerous cartridges are the high velocity ones loaded with a special powder and originally designed for wildfowling; they are unsafe in a gun with $2\frac{1}{2}$-inch chambers and a warning to this effect is printed on the cartridge boxes of reputable makes.

High velocity cartridges are sometimes spoken of with a good deal of ignorance. They are designed to provide greater hitting power at slightly longer ranges and especially at tough targets such as duck and geese. They contain more shot and so they should give a better pattern at the increased range, but they do not cover the distance between gun and target so much quicker than standard cartridges that their use can turn erstwhile misses into hits. Over 20 yards the mean velocity of the shot from a standard cartridge is 1,070 feet per second, while a high velocity cartridge is unlikely to give a better figure than 1,130 feet per second. To achieve this mean velocity the muzzle velocity has to be raised and this naturally causes greater recoil of the gun and perhaps discomfort to the man behind it. The striking energy of the pellets will be greater at 40 or 50 yards than when a standard cartridge is used and this is a benefit to the wildfowler but of no interest to the clay shooter. It is a fact that the pattern from any shotgun fails before the velocity, and therefore striking energy, of its pellets (which accounts for freak long-range shots at game), and so there is not much point in using high velocity cartridges, especially for shooting clays, unless the pattern can be preserved. And, unfortunately, high velocity loads often impair the pattern, although less so in tightly-choked guns than in those bored more openly. The user of these cartridges hopes that his pattern is improved because to the high velocity powder he adds more shot, 1¼-oz. instead of the 1⅛ or 1/16 normally used. Once again, to ensure good results, the gun should be pattern tested with the proposed cartridges before changing to them for serious competition, because otherwise the user may suffer a sore shoulder from the greater recoil and gain nothing of advantage as regards his gun's performance.

The calculated forward allowance for a target crossing at 40 m.p.h. at a range of 40 yards is about 4 inches less using a good high velocity cartridge than it is with a standard load, and such a small amount cannot make any appreciable difference in the swing required to put a clay pigeon in the 30-inch circle, even if it is only a small target about 4½ inches across. Confidence in one's equipment is essential to success, and if an Olympic Trench shooter really believes he can do better with high velocity cartridges he is justified in using them, but unhappily he may turn to them for no better reason than that he sees other people with them and he fears that they may be gaining some advantage over him. As always with guns and cartridges, you should fully understand the capabilities and limitations of any detail of your equipment before adopting it, and you ought to test it before using it in competition.

Returning to the most suitable gun for the game, we see that another reason for choosing a heavy one is that sooner or later the user will want to try the heavy shot load of 1¼-oz., and this will cause more recoil which will be less noticeable on the heavy gun. Barrel length should be 28 or 30 inch according to the user's build.

How do we kill these Olympic Trench birds? The detailed instruction cannot be very different from that given for Down-The-Line, except that any lead required will be greater and that the necessity for quick shooting is even more emphasised, in each case because of the extra speed of the targets. Come to No. 1 firing mark and take up your normal stance: above the middle of the group of three traps in front of you there is a mark on the ground and just beyond that you can expect to see your target. Mount your gun, lean forward and bend slightly downwards from the waist. You must expect the clay to go in virtually any direction away from you, perhaps skimming flat and close to the ground or perhaps rising up quite considerably. Line up your gun muzzles on that mark on the ground, concentrate hard and call 'Pull!'. From your experience of Down-The-Line shooting you will know how to compete with the type of target you are offered, be it a straight going-away shot or one quartering to a greater or lesser degree. You will not normally meet as much of a crossing shot as sometimes occurs at Down-The-Line but that does not mean that you can neglect forward allowance on the clays that go out to a flank. Swing fast, get ahead of the target and pull the trigger smartly and smoothly. Remember also that the rising birds are actually moving upward faster than they were on the D.T.L. layout and you must be sure to swing well up through them, with the movement coming from the hips and not only from the arms. It is fatally easy to miss these fast clays underneath.

When you move along to the other firing positions the procedure is the same, and you may find it unsettling at first to have only one shot at each position instead of having five as with Down-The-Line. From each numbered position you will see a mark on the ground for the group of three traps in front of you and this is where you must look for your target. Each shot from each of the five stations must be taken as an individual target, the only one, the most important one of the day, the one you are just about to kill. Because you have to move for each shot you must be sure to settle in correctly to the right stance, ready to take a shot at any likely angle. You should get into a rhythm of walking across to the next stand and quickly adopting the correct position for your shot. It is not quite true to say that 'there is no time to waste', but the whole sequence of competitors moving along the firing line and taking their shots moves smoothly, and if you lag behind you may be subconsciously bullied into calling for your next target before you are really ready for it.

The clays come into the shooter's view at about the level of his feet and for this reason there is a tendency to want to lower the body towards the line where the target first appears. Crouching, however, is not advised, it is not helpful and it must make for unsteadiness. A firm stance on a straight left leg provides the most certain steady platform for the gun. Many shooters make a slight bend of the left knee, after they have taken their aim and just before they call for their target; it may be an almost unconscious movement due to the desire to pick up the low target over the gun as soon as possible, and it is more noticeable among Down-The-Line shooters who are accustomed to a higher sighting plane than among experienced Trench competitors; you will see many expert shots standing normally upright as they prepare to mount the gun and then, as they do so, they just lean forward and bend a little at the waist : infinitely better style than any sort of leg bending, and far more likely to be followed by a smooth, unwavering swing with the gun muzzles never leaving the target's flight line. Some first-class shots take Olympic Trench birds without holding their guns to their shoulders as they call 'Pull'. They point the gun, and then drop it off the shoulder, not as far as a correct gun down position, but as far off as you would between shots at Skeet doubles. This shows that an upright stance and even a ready position with the gun off the shoulder can bring success, and so you should not follow other people's unusual non-standard styles merely because you think they are good shots and therefore their methods must be correct. Some odd styles are accompanied by straight shooting and if a man kills his birds it matters but little what style he adopts; but it is always better in the beginning to adopt standard methods and alter them only if you find the changes improve your accuracy. If you experience a strong desire to adopt the bent left knee position for the lower pick up of the Olympic Trench target, make the bend as slight as possible, but you are strongly advised to keep to the firm straight leg position for all shooting. (Plate 41.)

As you mount your gun at the mark on the ground over the three traps in front of you, remember that there is a considerable variation in the directions and elevations of all the possible targets. Hence the importance of a perfect pick up of the clay over the barrels and a stance that will enable you to follow its exact flight line whether this is high or low, straight away or off to one side. If your judgement of the line of flight is at fault your swing and lead will be wrong anyway, and only a large amount of luck will give you a kill. This applies to all forms of shooting, whether at clays or live game : collect the target over the gun barrels, keeping the muzzles between it and your eye, follow through the flight line from just behind the target, swing on and you must score a hit; if you miss you can be sure you were behind, and so for the second shot you should double your lead. Olympic Trench shooting is that extra bit more difficult than most types because of the high speed of the targets, the fact that they are receding and so increasing the range all the time, and because their direction is unpredictable.

Although you cannot say where your next target is going before it appears, you will realise that during a round of 25 birds you are likely to have some types of shot repeated, since there are only 15 possible ones in front of you. You will not know when to expect a repeat but you can profit from your mistakes by doing some self-criticism when you miss, and deciding what mistake you made; then you ought to be able to apply the necessary correction when you are confronted by the same target again. For instance, should you miss the right-hand angled clay from No. 4 stand you may realise that it was indeed at a broad angle across your front, requiring more lead than you gave, and it was also rising more steeply than you had reckoned when you tried to swing along its line of flight. If you could have that bird again immediately you would surely kill it the second time but of course that is not to be. You can, however, keep that shot in mind, not to the exclusion of everything else because you have to go on shooting the others, but sooner or later when you are back at No. 4 firing mark that right-hander will appear again and you should at once be able to pick it up correctly, apply that extra lead required and kill it. You may meet this particular target for the second time quite soon after you first missed it, or perhaps not at all in that round of 25 birds but later on in the series. The important point is that you can learn from your mistakes and take action to put matters right when the same circumstances recur.

The only times you can predict the course of the next target are when the referee declares 'No bird' because:

1. The clay breaks when it is thrown, provided that a

large enough piece of it goes in a recognisable direction.

2. The trap is fired before you call for your target.

3. You call, the bird fails to appear and as you lower your gun the trap goes off late.

In all these cases another target is allowed and it will be from the same trap that produced the 'No bird', so you know in advance where it is going. Such mistakes in operation are rare but if they do occur when you are in the line you can take advantage of them by concentrating on the known flight line of your repeated target, and probably by altering your point of aim from the mark over the traps to one side or other according to where you know the clay will go.

Olympic Trench competitions are occasions which may call for coloured clays; this is a decision for the Committee who will aim to use the most suitable colour according to the background. At the high speed and long ranges of these clays black may not show up as well as red or yellow, especially in a dull light. This matter is mentioned only for interest, and to show that although the Trench layout is designed to be difficult no one wants to make it impossibly so by using clays which become invisible!

The effect of wind is much the same as at Down-The-Line except that the strong Olympic traps can throw a clay for a greater distance before it is affected by the wind. If you shoot fast enough the wind ought not to worry you but, all the same, do not ignore it and take note, after you have shot one or two rounds, of any wind change which could alter some of the flight lines of the targets on subsequent rounds.

Study the rules before you shoot in a competition, and before you do even a practice round it is worth reading the I.S.U. Regulations which, among many other matters, include some succinct remarks about safety; they stress the need to carry guns unloaded and with the breech open, and magazine guns with the muzzle pointing up. Orders are clear, too, about precisely when guns may be loaded and when they must be unloaded, as when walking from No. 5 station to No. 1.

Olympic Trench is for experts at clay pigeon shooting but anyone interested in the sport may hope to improve, and as his standard moves into the top class he will wish to try something different. Another difference, and a recent innovation in the artificial target world is the ZZ plastic clay pigeon.

As a digression from Olympic Trench shooting a description of the ZZ may be of interest because it is likely to become popular as a way of sporting clay pigeon shooting, although it is not yet recognised as a form to be competed for at the major Championship meetings.

The ZZ clay, also called the Robot Pigeon, first appeared at Monte Carlo in 1963. It was produced to take the place of live pigeon shooting which had been banned by the Sovereign Prince; the ban, in what was once the world centre for live pigeon shooting, caused a financial loss in the Principality because the shooting clientele removed their valuable custom and shot their pigeons in Italy, chiefly at San Remo. The ZZ was designed to lure the customers back again and in this object it appears to be successful.

The ZZ has a white central disc similar in shape to a normal clay pigeon, but it is made of plastic. Protruding from the edge are two 'wings', slightly twisted to form the blades of a propeller. (See Plate 42.)

Shooting procedure is similar to that for live pigeon. There are five traps and the shooter faces these, standing on his handicap mark, and he checks with the puller that they are both ready. The puller then starts the five electric ejector motors in the traps, and when the target is called for he presses a button which operates a random selection device to set off one of the ejectors. The electric motor spins the Robot, which is loaded vertically, so that the propeller with its disc in the middle takes off horizontally, or nearly so. The view from the shooter is of a red blurr from the whirring propeller blades, with a white centre. The ZZ goes off very fast and soon flattens out, to turn the disc into a normal near-horizontal plane, but then it shoots off in any unexpected direction, performing the zig-zag which provides its identifying name.

ZZ's produce some tricky shooting and their erratic flight is not dissimilar to that of live pigeon. Although the whole target is bigger than a standard clay a pellet or three from the edge of the pattern going through the wings will not produce a kill, for which the central disc is required to fall away from the propellor or to be smashed completely. A pellet in the wings will make the ZZ swerve but will not knock it down, thus accentuating the similarity to shooting a live pigeon not very efficiently. What would have been an effective shot at a real bird will register on the Robot.

The handicap mark was mentioned two paragraphs back and it may be of interest to learn how this handicapping is sometimes evolved. Since shooting live pigeon or the Robots is very much a financial business, for the organisers and for the 'professionals' who reckon to win large cash prizes, the special rules, when enforced, are different from those applicable to a normal clay shooting competition. The newcomer finds he is handicapped as if he was an expert: right on the back mark, furthest from the traps! But then, as he spends more money on entrance fees he is moved forward, and the more he spends the closer he stands to the traps. Should he, however, win a prize he will be moved back again, the distance depending on the size of his prize; the whole thing is carefully worked out on a sliding scale to encourage competitors to spend money and to keep them shooting to try to improve their handicap and give themselves a chance of winning back some of their expenses. *Quel bon artifice!*

ZZ shooting could have a great future. It is certainly different from anything encountered with ordinary clays and it does not stir up the strong emotions that are roused among the 'anti's' by those who shoot live pigeon.

The technique for killing Robots is a combination of Olympic Trench allied to experience in the jinking behaviour of a real pigeon in flight. In reasonably still air the targets are not particularly difficult for a good shot, but in anything of a wind they pose a very interesting problem. The cost of the traps is high and it will be some time before many layouts are available, but the ZZ has already arrived in England and clay shooters throughout the world will no doubt soon be agitating to persuade their clubs to acquire the necessary equipment so that they may raise their guns to this fascinating newcomer to the sport.

Universal Trench is now shot as an economical way of practising for Olympic Trench. The layout consists of five traps placed in a trench. The traps can be set to throw clays on certain defined trajectories; but once having been set, they remain fixed during a shoot. After the 1968 Olympic Games, draft rules were adopted by the International Shooting Union for a new form of competition provisionally called Automatic Trap. A special trap is used, which continually weaves up and down, as well as from side to side, and fires off clays in whatever direction it happens to be pointing when the shot is called. The device is in use in some clubs, and is often known as Ball Trap.

CHAPTER SEVEN

SINGLE-BARREL
AND DOUBLE-RISE

THESE are the names given to two forms of competition which do not enjoy the same status and popularity as Down-The-Line or Skeet. They are sometimes run as concurrent events at the same Championship meeting, both being restricted to only one shot at each target on a Down-The-Line layout; in the first event single clays are thrown and in the other pairs.

In Single-Barrel shooting all the normal rules apply except that implicit in the title. This fulfils the dual purpose of reducing the cost to the competitors, who do not have to buy so many cartridges, and of fostering concentration and correct procedure among newcomers to the sport. It is better for a learner to have only one shot and to practise, with instruction if possible, than to blaze away with both barrels not knowing why he misses with either of them. There is often a temptation for a youngster to want to fire two shots when he first uses a double-barrelled gun, or a repeater for that matter, and when he tries it out, maybe at pigeon or rabbits, he behaves as if he thinks he is not really getting the most out of his gun unless he fires two shots. After a while, when he realises that cartridges cost money, he slows up his rate of fire. He is unaware of the basic object in having two barrels on a game gun which is to kill two birds without having to reload, not to have a second chance at one missed. In clay shooting at one target it is obviously sensible to have a second shot if

35. An Olympic Trench, with its battery of 15 traps. The marks over the centre of each group of three can be seen on the corrugated iron roof.

36. The trappers down in their trench. These traps need re-cocking by hand after each release and the three men are kept busy.

37. A newer type of Olympic Trench, made of concrete.

38. An electric trap in an Olympic Trench. This is the right hand one of a group of three and it has just released its clay to the left. These traps cock themselves automatically and only need reloading afterwards.

39. The Olympic Trench firing line, No. 2 shooting, the sixth man walking along the back from No. 5 to No. 1 stand.

40. The man on the right fires, the referee stands by him holding a hooter to use in case of a miss, and another shooter moves from his stand, carrying his gun in the open position. The numbers in the background are on a rifle range.

41.   A good position. Firm left leg, cheek well onto the comb, a good hold
with his left hand. The next shooter stands ready to take his turn.

42.
A ZZ Robot Pigeon. It has a white centre and
red propellor blades. Total length is 12 inches.
This one has had a chip or two knocked out
of the wings; it was not killed.

43.
When shooting doubles he lowers the butt as he
swings from his first target to the second. He is
picking up the line over the gun muzzles.

you miss with the first but in the early stages, when one is primarily learning to shoot, it is preferable to fire only one barrel and then, when the result is a miss, something can be done to check on what went wrong. Two quick, erratic shots help not at all to discover the cause of missed targets but one steady shot does, even if the only critic available is the shooter himself.

A good way to start clay shooting is for a few friends to obtain an ordinary single trap and set it up in a field, with the trapper protected by straw bales and the five Down-The-Line firing marks placed 16 yards from the trap. When learning to shoot this way, however, only one barrel should be fired at each target if any instructional benefit is to be obtained. The keen beginner should soon join a club where he will find an automatic trap and where he will learn a considerable amount by watching others; it is advisable for him to start by giving the impression that he knows nothing about clay shooting, when he will find that the other members will be friendly and helpful in teaching him. The important point, often not appreciated by the novice or those trying to instruct him, is that he will learn more if he initially restricts himself to firing only one barrel.

Perhaps the main object of having a Single-Barrel Championship is to provide some variety in the season's events and to offer another competition after the main ones, (D.T.L., Skeet, Olympic Trench), have been completed. Shortly after the 1939-45 war cartridges were in short supply and at all the big meetings the one barrel rule was enforced. This temporary restriction had an interesting effect: many of the competitors who had been accustomed to using two barrels found that they were upset by being limited to one. The good shots probably required their second barrel only five times in a round of a hundred birds but now they found they were needing it perhaps twenty times. This was because, being limited to one shot, they tried to take more care over it, knowing that there was no second chance to back it up; consequently they altered their timing with disastrous results; they had forgotten that making sure is fatal. In all forms of shooting, once you are committed to the shot you must take it without delay for if you hang on that little bit longer, trying too hard, you will almost certainly miss. 75% of the success of a shot comes from correct preparation for it, from a correct stance to good gun mounting; a pause at the critical moment preceding the pulling of the trigger will upset everything.

As an experienced shot, if you enter a Single-Barrel event you must strive to get your mental attitude right. The shooting is the same as normal Down-The-Line, and so there is no new problem there; you have to persuade yourself that the loss of the second barrel matters not the least, you are going to kill all your birds first shot, anyway. When you go to your firing mark be determined to shoot quickly, just as you normally do at D.T.L., and make certain that you do not alter your timings: think to yourself 'Gun up—ready—call for the target—note its course and collect it over the barrels—shoot, instantly!' If you watch others at a Single-Barrel event you will soon notice that nearly all the missed shots are due to the shooter dwelling in the aim, trying to take extra care for which there is no time once the clay is on its way.

Double-rise is a somewhat ponderous phrase for what are colloquially known simply as doubles; the term doubles can, however, apply to any pair of clays released together, as at Skeet, or thrown towards the shooter as on a Sporting layout, while the Double-rise we are considering is from a Down-The-Line trap. The mechanism for continuously altering the direction in which the trap faces is locked, and consequently it

[142]

always operates at set horizontal and vertical angles; two clays are loaded on the carrrier plate, one in front of the other, and when the trap is fired one clay goes to the right and one to the left, at angles of about 45° to the line from No. 3 firing mark to the trap. The flight line of the clays is constant throughout the competition but the shooters move position along the line of firing marks, as with normal Down-The-Line. A round is generally 10 pairs, two at each of the firing marks, making 20 birds, each of which may only be shot at once, and so there is a slight similarity to Single-Barrel shooting.

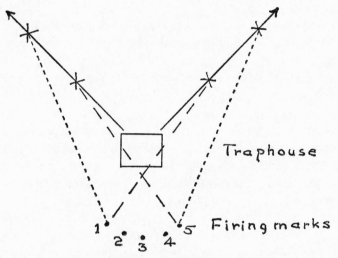

Fig. VI. – Double-rise

The first shot from No. 1 and No. 5 firing marks is shown by a broken line - - - - - -, and the second by a dotted line . . . . . . x shows the point along the flight path where the clay is broken.

It does not matter in which order the doubles are shot but it is usually easier to take the going-away bird first, as this can be shot very quickly, and then you will have more time to swing onto the second bird. Study Figure VI and you will

[143]

see that from No. 1 firing mark the right-hand of the pair of clays presents very nearly a straight away shot which is quickly increasing its range, and this is another reason for catching it as soon as possible; the diagram shows the first shot taken at the right-hand clay and the second at the left-hand. When you come to shoot the left-hand bird it will be at an angle to which you are accustomed from normal D.T.L., but it will be further away; with a regulation trap you should be able to kill the first bird at about 30 to 32 yards and by the time you have caught up with the second it will have travelled 35, perhaps even 40 yards. At any time after about 34 yards the clay flattens out its trajectory and starts to drop and for this you must watch very carefully. Your second bird will need more lead than you might expect and if it has begun to drop you must swing down under it. This is a new situation since always before you have striven to catch the clay early in its flight, while it was still rising. For a real bird which is crossing or quartering and also dropping, the gun should be swept down under its throat, just as we spoke of swinging above the neck of a rising bird, and the same applies when the target is a clay. The line of flight is not a straight line but an arc curving downwards which emphasises the need to keep the barrels swinging under its throat if we are to avoid over-shooting.

You may think that throughout this instruction there is too much exhortation to shoot fast; it must, however, be apparent that the good gun mounting leading to fast gun handling does provide the shooter with an easier shot than if he wastes time while the shooting problem in front of him is growing in severity. Such is the case with the second shot at doubles, which becomes more difficult the longer you wait. You may hear tales of excessive lead being required but this only applies to the man who is late with his shot, and remember that your

[144]

gun is swinging just about as fast as you can make it from the first clay to the second, and so a reasonable lead should be enough. If you miss your targets, especially the second one, do not slow up your timing because by doing so you will never become a good doubles shooter; you may catch that second clay at long range occasionally but for real consistent success you must kill it as early as possible; it is better to keep to regular fast timing for the two shots and sometimes miss the second one, and with experience you will soon score more kills if you keep to the standard drill.

In order to help you to speed up the second shot you can, when practising doubles, keep the gun at the shoulder after the first shot while you swing across to the other one, but you ought to do this only about half a dozen times. The suggestion is made only to show you that the second barrel can be fired very soon after the first and it does not matter very much if the early shots are misses. You ought to be able to prove to yourself that this procedure is wrong because :

1. You will find that the recoil of the first shot sometimes displaces the correct fitting of the butt to your shoulder and your cheek on the comb.

2. With the gun still at your shoulder as you swing to the second clay there is a tendency to look away from the barrels towards your next target.

3. You cannot so easily pick up the exact line of flight of the second clay if you keep your gun up.

A more satisfactory way of gun handling is to take the butt off the shoulder between shots, as you were advised to do with Skeet doubles; immediately after the first shot, which is not fully completed until you have followed through for that extra split second with your cheek still on the stock, you lower the butt a few inches; then pivot round and pick up the line

[145]

of the new target over the muzzles, mount the gun again and shoot. This drill will help you to appreciate more precisely the course of the second clay and it will ensure that the gun is mounted correctly for the shot. (Plate 43.)

All the targets are following consistent courses and so you can adopt your stance and aiming point accordingly. You should stand with your front, 12 o'clock in Figure I, midway between the paths of the two clays; you should not stand to face the line of the first clay and so have a considerable amount of pivoting to do for the second, nor should you adopt a bent left knee nor any winding-up sort of crouch. At No. 1 firing mark your front would be slightly to the left of the traphouse, and from a normal upright stance you can pivot about a half turn to the right for your first shot, and when you take the second one you will be about half a turn to the left, from your original front.

Because you know in advance where your targets are going, unlike normal Down-The-Line, you can adjust your aiming point. Instead of aiming at the centre of the traphouse you should, from No. 1 stand for the right-hand clay, aim at the top right-hand corner of the traphouse, which will help you to pick up the target over the barrels an important fraction of a second earlier. This aiming point will move across the top of the traphouse as you go along the firing marks, and you may find you can point a little above the traphouse roof because you know the clays are elevating at quite a high angle. Do not, however, point the barrels so high that they prevent you seeing the clay at the earliest possible moment. A sharp-eyed man with quick reactions and much experience of Down-The-Line clays can see them only inches away from the trap, especially when they are on a pre-determined course, but a newcomer to the sport or someone with slower sight is unable to register the clay until it has travelled several yards.

[146]

At No. 2 firing mark, adopting the principle of taking the going-away bird first, you will again shoot the right-hand clay and then the left. At No. 3 mark you are centrally placed and can take either bird first according to which way you find easier for that quick swing on the second shot; most people prefer to take the right-hand shot first because the big swing to the left comes more naturally, rather than the other way round. At No. 4 and No. 5 firing marks you take the left-hand clay first. Remember that the argument in favour of this method of selecting the order in which the targets are taken is based on shooting the easier one first and the one which is more of a receding shot; any delay will allow it to reach a greater range than would the other of the pair during the same amount of time. Clay doubles, however, do not always fly precisely as planned. A fault in the trap may cause one clay to go higher than the other and a strong cross wind most certainly will, since it will push up the clay going into it and flatten the trajectory of the other one. You should therefore watch the prevailing conditions all the time and consider which is the better target to take first. If they are flying at appreciably different heights it will usually be advisable to shoot the low clay first because it is difficult to swing quite considerably down again for the second shot, this being an an unnatural movement rarely found in any form of shooting, whether at game or clays.

Some doubles shooters always take the same bird first at each firing mark and perhaps they reckon this saves them the trouble of pondering on the problem of the order in which to shoot each pair. You will have more chance of success, however, if you think carefully about it, at any rate until you reach the expert class. A brilliant shot was once shooting doubles and he overheard the spectators talking behind him :

[147]

"You see," said one of them, "he always takes the going-away shot first and then the crosser."

"Yes," replied his friend. "That makes it easier, doesn't it?"

On his next pair the marksman shot the crosser first, followed by the going-away bird, and he listened again to the two spectators, and the argument that began between them. At the end of the series one of them asked him why he kept changing in his selection of targets and he airily explained that he liked to change his swing and put a bit of variety into the proceedings. He was an expert, he was right on form and he could probably have shot the lot from a sitting position, but no one out of his class should base the selection of the order in which the clays are shot on nothing more than a wish to try a little leg-pulling on the spectators.

There is one most pointed moral to this story, for the average shooter. And that is to deplore the fact that the spectators' conversation was overheard in the first place. 'Silence' is the rule behind the firing line, often emphasised by a notice board but frequently ignored, and while you are shooting you must concentrate on the job and strive to pay no attention to what goes on behind you. If you cannot help hearing what is being said wear ear-plugs; many trapshooters do so, and not only to help them from being partially deafened by the continual report of the gun.

Recent medical evidence shows that permanent damage to the ears can result from the noise of firing a shotgun. Clay shooters, especially, should seriously consider using one of the several aids on the market. The large muff type is probably the best, although game shooters would doubtless prefer one of the less conspicuous ear-plugs.

Double-rise is often reckoned to be the most difficult of all clay shooting but this is a point about which most followers of the sport will never tire of arguing. Lists of averages and scores at the main competitions certainly give the impression that doubles are more difficult, but a reason for the lower scores could be a lack of practice because doubles are not so popular; the number of entries at Championship meetings is very much less for Double-rise than for Down-The-Line, and this is partly due to the fact that some D.T.L. specialists prefer not to compete at doubles because they think that to do so would upset their timing for their favourite event.

One fact that helps to make doubles easier is that all the targets follow the same flight path, except in unusual wind conditions or if the trap is not properly adjusted. When misses occur they are nearly always due to certain definite reasons which are worth considering.

The first shot, especially if it is taken at the going-away bird, is often missed underneath; the clay is rising fast and the barrels must be swung well up through it. Above all, it must not be taken as a snapshot which can happen because the shooter is hurrying to move on to the second target. Shooting fast does not mean shooting in a slapdash manner and good timing infers a steady, regular movement with no time wasted but no flurried haste; it calls for perfect co-ordination between eye, gun and body, which you may think is easy to write about but not so easy to achieve! Patience and practice, however, can work wonderful improvements in what is, after all, good basic style, that prerequisite of success at any sport or game dependent on an instrument such as rod or gun, racquet or club.

Do not look away from your gun barrels after the first shot. As always, the muzzles must remain in a line between your eye and the target and if you break the line by turning your head to see the second clay you will have difficulty in re-adjusting it correctly.

On the second shot do not dwell in the aim. Swing onto it and shoot, and if you miss you are at least trying to do the right thing. Experience will turn the lost birds into kills.

Learn where to aim for each target from each firing mark and where on its flight path you can expect to hit it. Remember especially to pivot from the hips and not to swing your arms, leaving your body behind. Watch for this as a reason for missing because in your keenness to take the second shot quickly you may fall into the habit of throwing the gun across with your arms only.

Concentration is even more important at doubles than it was at singles because you have to think of the two targets. While taking your stance you should be preparing for both the shots but then, as you bring up your gun for the first you must concentrate only on that one and not think again of the second until the first is killed. Otherwise your mind will be trying to make you do two things at once and you will lose both birds.

Confidence is particularly necessary and it can only be built up by success, probably obtained by some fairly light-hearted practice. When you do this make up your mind that shooting is for fun, that you are going to enjoy it and prove that the difficulties are not so very great. Under these conditions it is surprising how soon doubles shooting can be learnt. When you have achieved a fair measure of success you will at the same time have improved your game shooting.

Some of the requisite confidence stems from using the right equipment and as far as the type of gun is concerned the choice is wide, with the proviso that the gun should be fairly tightly choked. The same requirements pertain as for the Down-The-Line gun discussed in Chapter 4, but a number of shooters who have a favourite side-by-side game gun prefer to use it for doubles rather than the under-and-over which is so often a first choice for D.T.L. The arguments in favour of side-by-side barrels were discussed in Chapter 5 when it was pointed out that their broader sighting plane is an advantage for crossing shots; a suggested reasoning against the over-and-under gun for the quick swing through a wide arc which occurs in doubles shooting is that the depth of the two barrels offers more air resistance, and this feature is exaggerated when there is a side wind. Such an argument is not as far-fetched as it might appear, as any angler will know if he has experienced the markedly noticeable effect of wind on fishing rods, when a thick one requires more effort to wield than a thin one. Use the weapon which suits you and do not change to something else, perhaps a pump gun, merely because you see someone shooting well with it.

Take note of the rules at any Single-Barrel or Double-rise competition for which you are entering and remember that at the doubles you are allowed only one shot at each target. Scoring at Single-Barrel is straight forward kills to count, and for doubles it is usually 5 points for killing both birds of a pair and 2 points for killing either one of them. Double-rise certainly makes a spectacular game and you ought to try it whenever the opportunity occurs.

CHAPTER EIGHT

SPORTING   CLAYS

A SPORTING layout makes the maximum use of natural features of the countryside and its object is to simulate live targets. The greater the variety of shots offered the more entertaining will be the shooting but a good layout requires plenty of space to allow for safety in all directions, and it needs a large staff of trappers, judges and scorers.

With sufficient equipment clay targets can be used to imitate walked-up game, such as grouse or partridge, and also driven birds, sometimes fairly low and sometimes very high like a rocketing pheasant. They can represent pigeon flying out of a wood or crossing a gap between two trees, and teal springing up off a pond, and there is a special clay to bowl along the ground like a running rabbit. It is rare to find all these types of shot on one layout but even with a restricted choice it is a popular form of shooting, as is shown by the fact that at the Sporting Championship of Great Britain the numbers of entries have been continually increasing, and were 700 in 1981. See Figure VII for a suggested layout.

The shooting rules include 'silent rise' for the release of the clays, which means that the referee signals with an electric buzzer to the trapper when the shooter is ready but the latter does not call 'Pull'. Taking aim or addressing the target before its release is not permitted and when the competitor is ready to shoot the gun must be in the Gun Down position,

■ denotes a **trap**

⊙ denotes a gun

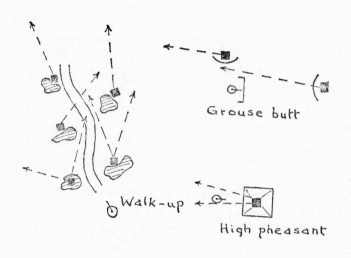

Grouse butt

Walk-up

High pheasant

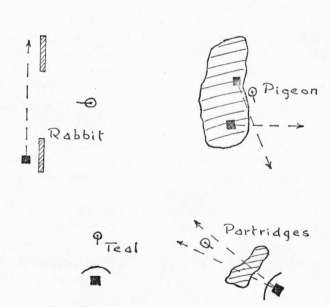

Rabbit

Pigeon

Teal

Partridges

FIG. VII. – EXAMPLE OF SPORTING LAYOUT

with the toe of the butt visible below his elbow. Guns must not be of a larger bore than 12 and cartridges are limited to $1\frac{1}{8}$-oz. of shot; a referee, incidentally, is empowered to inspect cartridges if he suspects anyone is cheating by using a bigger shot load. At driven birds both the shots of a pair must be taken in front and only one barrel is allowed at each. Sometimes the clays may be fairly close together, for they are not thrown at widely different angles as at Double-rise, and if they are both broken with one shot the score is 'No bird', and the pair are taken again. If one bird of a driven pair is killed but the other breaks as it leaves the trap the kill counts but the pair must be repeated; on the repeat the shooter must fire at both clays and it does not matter if he misses the first one because he has already scored his kill there, but for a kill to count on the second he must hit it with his second shot. This is important and failure to understand the rule results in a shooter firing only one barrel at the repeated pair and so losing a point.

Safety rules are most important, particularly because the layout is spread over a large area and there are usually many spectators wandering around. Guns may be loaded only when on a firing point under control of a referee and they must be unloaded as soon as the series is finished. All trappers should have a red flag which they can hold up to signal for shooting to stop if they need to come out of their protective housing for any reason, such as to collect more clays.

Sporting clays cannot be quite the same as the real thing but they can make a very fair imitation and the shooting technique is the same as for game. Critics sometimes say 'How can you claim these clay targets are like a real bird when they start to slow down after a few yards?' Anybody who thinks this and assumes that the slowing down will make the target easier to hit almost invariably misses behind when he tries to prove his point. If the clay is taken at the proper time and in the correct place it will not have slowed down and will, in fact, be easier to hit.

How closely the shoot can represent live targets depends on the site available, and if this is large enough a very good lay-out can be arranged. Some years ago a shoot was held over an area covering 100 acres. The competitors started by walking along a strip of scrub in which were several traps which released clays at varying angles, some high and some low, and the uneven ground was a test for correct footwork. They then came to a shallow quarry and as they stood at the bottom, driven partridges flew over the lip, as singles and as pairs and sometimes four at a time, to make it more interesting. From there they walked across a field where grouse appeared in pairs, one approaching and another going away behind, and then they were directed to another quarry. On the way a teal shot up from an imaginary pond and, admittedly unnaturally, this was followed by several more doing the same thing. In the quarry, which was deep and surrounded by bushes, they had to compete with some high pheasants which came unpredictably from either side, sometimes one at a time and sometimes in pairs; this was a particularly 'sporting' stand because, the whole layout being unseen beforehand, the shooter did not know from which direction to expect his next target. There followed a walk of about a quarter of a mile back to base, with odd birds jumping up from behind bushes and a couple of crossing pigeon going through a gap in some trees, and finally some rabbits bolting across a short open space and disappearing behind a bank. This shoot was organised by a club with ample resources of equipment and members willing to help as referees and trappers; it was done for entertainment, which was much appreciated by the competitors, but it entailed a great deal of hard work. It involved a

[155]

fairly considerable walk, of about three-quarters of a mile, some of it uphill, and it was designed to be undertaken as one continuous whole, a fairly strenuous one and, in its way, not unlike the cross-country event at the Badminton horse trials. Stamina was under test as well as shooting skill, and an intrinsically good shot might well find himself lower down on the final list of results than a normally poorer performer who combined a little luck with a superior ability to take every variety of shot with composure and a reserve of strength.

A Sporting layout designed for serious competition must be reasonably compact, with the different stands more or less centrally placed and facing outwards. There is then not very much walking for the competitors to do and they can choose the order in which they take each type of target, and have a rest between stands whenever they wish. This somewhat easier arrangement does at least ensure that the best performer, at Sporting clays, has every chance of winning, which is an essential object in the organisation of a Championship meeting. Shooting Sporting clays can be made more realistic than is sometimes the case but only if the primary object is to provide the shooters with some amusement; as soon as a serious competitive element is introduced, with some much-valued prizes at stake, the performance inevitably assumes some of the set drill, with scrupulous fairness to all, that is associated with any other type of clay shooting competition. But that does not alter the fact that the targets themselves closely represented the sporting birds after which they are named.

An ordinary side-by-side game gun is the most suitable weapon for these targets, with a boring of improved cylinder and $\frac{1}{2}$ or $\frac{3}{4}$-choke, but a repeater or over-and-under may be used if preferred; the most important feature about the gun is that it should be one which suits the user and which he would

44. The 120ft. tower at a shooting School, used here for "rocketing pheasants" in a Sporting Competition. The shooter is using a side-by-side game gun and he favours a good long left reach, and his weight is well on the left leg. He killed his bird.

45.
"High pheasants" at a gun club's Sporting layout. The trap is fixed in the tree against which the ladder is placed. Two clays have just been released, caught by the camera but the shooter has not yet been able to mount his gun. This is difficult shooting.

46.
Taking a "high pheasant" at a game-keepers' clay shoot. This is a good position and the weight is not as far back as at first appears. The clay has been broken and this is the continuation of the swing.

Page 158

47. The "springing teal" has sprung so quickly that the young shot has not yet registered it. The trap is beyond the word "Teal" in the photograph and the clay flies straight up between the two trees.

48.
"Driven partridges" come over the bush and on over the shooter's head. The scorers sit behind, and get showered with bits of broken clay.

49.
A good stance for another "driven partridge." The shooter has short arms and so his left hand does not reach out very far along the fore-end.

50. While the gun club runs its competition one corner of the layout is reserved for instructing novices. The shooter here has an awkward left arm, the elbow looks uncomfortable and the hand position is too far back.

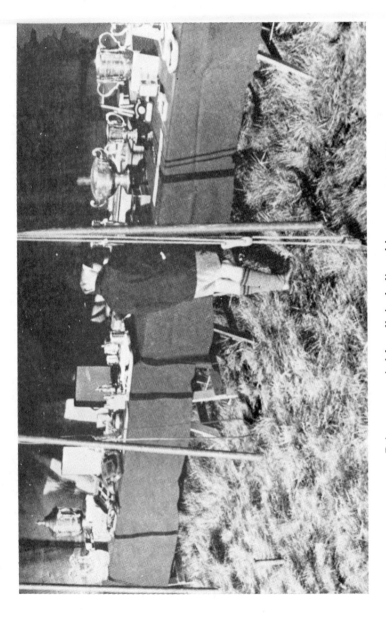

51. Prizes are envied by all, including this young spectator.

choose for normal game shooting. As regards cartridges, the main decision concerns the shot size and, because the target is small, sizes 7, 8 and 9 are in demand rather than the standard game size of 6. At recent Championship meetings 7's have been the most popular shot and they might well be taken as the standard for this type of shooting, with 8's recommended for an open-bored gun. Size 9 is scarcely worth bothering with unless you can prove, by careful test, that they are capable of giving an improved pattern; they have the disadvantage of being comparatively scarce and sometimes unobtainable.

Now we should study the different types of target, and how to shoot them, starting with the walked-up birds. In the descriptions that follow it must be borne in mind that all Sporting layouts differ according to the lie of the land and the resources available, but the principles of how to deal with the shooting problems remain the same. When walking-up, the competitor moves along a grass path and the clays are thrown from traps concealed in bushes on either side; they may be singles or doubles, high or low, but they all fly more or less away from the shooter. He is followed by a referee and the trapper who releases the pre-loaded traps by remote control. If only about half a dozen traps are used a competitor waiting his turn can watch someone else shooting and learn what type of shot he can expect. The better walk-up has as many as thirty traps and only some of these are needed for each series; this provides variety and keeps the customers guessing.

The most important point when walking-up is correct footwork, and the clay shooter who is accustomed to a level concrete platform on which to stand is faced with a new problem; indeed, so also is the game shot who is only used to driven birds. When walking it is essential to stop before you try to shoot; although this may seem obvious, failure to stand

[163]

still and properly balanced is the cause of many misses. You should walk naturally just as you would when walking-up partridges or grouse; do not try any peculiar creeping or limping walk, with the right leg permanently behind the left, because it is a disadvantage to be caught with your left foot on the ground; when walking normally you can take a quick pace with the left foot as a target appears and place it exactly in the correct direction. When a target appears place your left foot firmly on the ground, towards 1 o'clock in Figure I, the target being at 12 o'clock. Do not try to mount the gun *as* your foot comes to the ground and most certainly do not try to shoot with the right leg in front. Lean forward onto that left leg and flick off the safety catch as you put the muzzles on the target, with the butt still down. Three things happen simultaneously : left foot on the ground, safety catch off, muzzles on the target.

To continue, pivot the body in the direction in which the clay is moving, with the muzzles closing up on the bird as the gun is brought up to the shoulder. On the instant that shoulder and cheek are locked onto the stock you should press the trigger, the swing carrying the gun through the flight line; at short range, 15 to 20 yards, no noticeable forward allowance will be necessary but at longer ranges, especially for a partly crossing shot, you will need to open out a little in front of the bird, bearing in mind the picture you have associated with similar shots before. There will be no tendency to stop or slow the swing if the feet and body positions are correct. After each shot you continue walking, remembering that the first thing to do on seeing a fresh target is to place your left foot in the proper position to deal with it; if a clay bobs up as your right foot is passing the left you must complete that pace and take another short one with the left foot before you start to mount the gun. If you have never done any walking-up before, or done it incorrectly, you ought to practise walking with a gun and stopping every few yards to acquire the feel of placing your feet correctly for targets in front and to either side.

A point to note about walked-up clays is that the rules normally permit both barrels to be fired at any target, either a single or one of a pair. When you have finished the walk you will collect your score card from the referee and move on to another stand, but you do not have to follow any particular order on your way round the course.

A good layout includes driven grouse but to do this properly a butt must be made. One trap faces the butt, about 35 yards out in front and another is alongside the butt arranged to fire to the rear; both have protective plates in front of them. The front trap sends a bird more or less over the butt while the second clay represents a grouse that has come through the line of guns from the front and is escaping behind. So here we have a problem which requires the shooter to move his feet to turn round between taking a shot in front and one behind.

The way to take these two grouse is to stand facing the trap in front, with a normal stance, straight left leg and the weight forward over the left hip, with the gun held as in Plate 9. Your eye looks past the end of the barrels at a point in the air above the trap shield where you expect the target to appear. When you see the fast-moving clay you will find that the muzzles are slightly left behind it; pivot the body to left or right, carrying the left hand and the gun with it; mount the gun so that the barrels smoothly overtake the bird and fire when just in front of it. The target will probably not go directly overhead because that shot will be tested on another stand; the usual practice is for it to cross the imaginary line of butts about 10 yards to a flank. We are shooting grouse,

[165]

remember, from a butt and therefore you must take the shot in front of the butt and not swing through the line and shoot out to the side where, in real grouse shooting, you would endanger the occupants of neighbouring butts.

On your first shot the second clay is released. You should then lower the stock from your shoulder and, because of the extra safety requirement, the muzzles should be raised to a nearly vertical position as you turn for the second barrel. Only when you have turned sufficiently to be past the line of butts are the barrels brought down so that they drop in behind the new target, and you can follow through and fire when you have opened out the necessary lead. The turn is a vital part of this second shot; it may be to right or left but the procedure is the same. As you fire you must place your foot well in front of where the target is at that instant; the foot should be far enough round to point towards where the bird will be killed and your body and gun then swing round to this position; at the moment of firing you are perfectly balanced with the gun and arms centrally over the left hip. The principle is that in the instant of turning your gun is behind the target but rapidly catching it up, and your feet are placed, in anticipation of the shot, ahead of the direction in which gun and eye are momentarily facing. The right foot is not moved off the ground while you pivot round on the ball of the foot. It is quite wrong to start by facing the second trap and hope you will be able to take the front clay and the rear one without moving the feet.

The rear trap is generally about ten yards away from the butt and this displacement ensures that its target is not a straight going-away shot, but the unwary shooter sometimes assumes it is and misses because he gives no sideways lead; in fact, quite a considerable lead is needed. As you actually fire this second shot you should be in a perfect position, well

[166]

balanced and with the weight on your left leg and centrally placed towards your target; this means that the clay, compared with the position of your feet, really is at 12 o'clock in Figure I and your swing can easily be carried on; it will be hopelessly impaired if you try to throw arms and gun across your body and shoot over your shoulder.

Turning for the shot behind is not difficult but it does require practice, and if you lack experience you should do some dry practice to learn the feel of co-ordinating the movements of the gun and your feet.

You may see some competitors at this stand moving their guns round from front to rear without raising the barrels to a safe position. This is fundamentally wrong if a genuine attempt is being made to simulate shooting grouse from a butt, and the rules ought to stipulate that such behaviour merits disqualification. You are advised to make the turn correctly and it will not cost you anything even in time, because the right shooting technique, quite apart from safety, is to take the gun butt off your shoulder between the two shots.

In order to have some high birds included in the round a trap can be fixed in a tree (Plate 45), or the competitors can be placed down in a hollow, perhaps using a quarry or a cliff. If the competition is being held at a Shooting School there will probably be a steel tower available as a permanent fixture and this is a great asset to the organisers. The tower will probably be about 80 ft. tall but it is difficult to fix a trap higher than about 40 ft. in a tree. A high pheasant in real life is seldom more than 100 ft. up and a rising clay from an 80 ft. tower is not much less than that by the time it goes over the gun.

It is usual to have a few single clays followed by pairs, and they may come straight overhead or slightly to one side or the other. To shoot them you should adopt a normal stance and, as the gun muzzles follow the line of flight of the target, you should move your body forward and reach up as if you were trying to sweep the clay out of the sky. The pivoting upward comes from the joint of the left hip and you must never sway off it to the side nor go back with your weight on the right leg because this would completely block your swing. The right heel should be raised off the ground. When the target is overhead it is out of sight behind the barrels at the moment of firing but you must not stop the swing to see if your shot has connected; push the gun up to the vertical and beyond, although it is actually fired before the clay reaches an overhead position. Do not tip your head backward except in conjunction with the bending movement of your body. (Plate 46.)

The height of these targets makes them appear to be slower than is really the case and they need a definite forward allowance. The speed of your swing is governed by the apparent speed of the clay to produce a smooth rhythmic shot, and this rhythm must be maintained. If you miss you should increase the lead, which is easier to do if the clay goes a bit to one side of you as you can then see your target as you fire; for the incoming overhead bird you should strive to pick it up over the muzzles as soon as possible after it leaves the trap and then you will have time and space to blot it out with the barrels well before it comes over you. If you fail to collect it early there will be no room to swing ahead for the necessary lead. Some people believe in swinging faster than usual in order to keep ahead of the target, but when using this method it is not possible to judge just how fast each swing is nor how much lead is obtained. You can watch the trap's protective shield, or the top of the tree if it is hidden, for the earliest possible sight of the clay and if you keep to a steady follow through for every shot you can appreciate when your barrels blot out the target and when you pull the trigger, this being a measurement of lead, even though you cannot see the target at the moment of firing. When the clays are slightly to one side you can see them as you fire and then you can determine your picture of the amount of lead, and you can increase it when necessary. For these shots not directly overhead your body and shoulders should pivot squarely from the hips.

When you shoot the doubles, both clays thrown together, it is most important that you treat the first as one single target, for if you think of two the first shot will probably be too quick and erratic. Make up your mind to shoot one at a time and choose for the first shot the one which first catches your eye. Never start to follow one and then change to the other. After the first shot, take the butt off your shoulder, be sure you do not drop the muzzles at the same time, and transfer them to the tail of the second pheasant. Replace the butt, swing through the bird and shoot. You are only allowed one shot at each target so pay no attention to whether you have hit the first, but immediately carry on with the second. You have to be quick on these doubles and any adjustment of your picture for the necessary amount of lead will have to be made while you are taking the singles.

Most Sporting layouts cannot show their pheasants at a greater height than about 25 yards and although this is not a long shot when taken nearly horizontally it looks quite high when straight up in the air. Sometimes, however, there may be available a really high tower, 120 ft. tall, which is 40 yards before the clays have risen off their trap, a rocketing pheasant and a high enough bird for anyone. (Plate 44.)

When you try the high tower you will immediately see how slowly the clays seem to be flying, especially if you are used to killing those quick birds out of a Down-The-Line trap. This apparent speed is most deceptive and it calls for a conscious effort of will to make yourself pull out to the necessary amount of forward allowance. As with the lower pheasants, your speed of swing is governed by the apparent speed of the clay and a considerable lead really is necessary. If you miss with the first shot double the lead on the next one, and if that misses double it again; do not be afraid of missing in front because that is almost impossible, as you may judge from a couple of stories which follow a little later.

It is usual to have some singles at the high tower, followed by pairs and these may be released together, going out side by side, or they may come one behind the other. In either case you should take the butt off your shoulder after the first shot and transfer the muzzles to the second target. If the second clay is following the first you must go back and pick it up from behind as you did with the first, and you have to be careful not to meet it and so lose the rhythm of swinging through its tail and forcing the gun out in front. Each shot should follow the same sequence of collecting the target from behind and following through. Incidentally, you may see people wandering about near the high tower, holding clays with one or two shot holes through them and complaining that they hit their target and were not credited with a kill. The shots were, of course, on the outside edge of the pattern and would not have killed a real pheasant, and so it is perfectly reasonable that they should not score a point in the competition. The rules insist that a visible piece shall be seen to break off the clay.

If there is a wind at the high tower it can make the birds curl, like real pheasants. You can ignore the effect of the wind on the shot but the sideways drift of the clay introduces an appreciable problem. With a pheasant in a cross wind it is sound technique to swing through the downwind wing tip in-

stead of through the bird's body and head, but that little
black clay has no wings to give us a guide. The best you can
do is to note carefully the flight line of the clay and swing
your gun through on arc instead of a straight line. This will
mean that if, for instance, the clay starts on a course a little to
your left, and a strong wind is blowing from that side, your
swing will be to the left and up a little more than had the
flight line been straight; if the clay starts to your right it will
be blown further that way and as the raised barrels follow
it they will have to be swung down slightly to follow its apparent path. This is difficult shooting and it emphasises the need
to break the target as early in its flight as possible before
the wind can influence it very much.

The amount of forward allowance necessitated by a long
range shot should not be measured in yards or feet. It can be
calculated, given the range and speed of the target, but such
figures are worthless in practice. No one can judge such specific distances in the air and in any case the lead required by
any one man depends on his own speed of swing and his timing in pulling the trigger. Two experienced shots once went
to a Shooting School because they had been missing long-
range crossing birds, particularly high pheasants. Each shot
at several clays and missed them behind, as the instructor
could see. After he had been told several times to swing further ahead one of them started to break his clays and he then
exclaimed, "Now I've got it, I can go on hitting them like
that!" And he killed six in a row. When the instructor asked
him what sort of lead he was giving these high birds he said,
"Ah, I know exactly now. It's a good ten feet."

The other visitor to the school also began missing behind
but he was helped by the instructor until he was hitting practically every target. He was very pleased and said that at last
he knew just what to do to kill them. When asked what allow-

[171]

ance he gave he replied, "Well, I thought one could shoot them just by swinging and firing as the gun passed them. But I see that one must get the gun in front. I reckon I give them nine inches lead."

From these two examples you will see that both shooters were right in their personal pictures of how they saw the target as they pulled the trigger, because they both killed consistently. But when they were asked to translate what they saw into a measurable distance their answers were remarkably different. Your picture, for any shot, is your own and you must stick to it. If you miss long-range shots open out your picture until you are successful; make yourself hold onto the swing after you have fired and resist any temptation to lift your cheek off the stock to see the result. Never, when you know a big lead is necessary, try to mount the gun and then swing past the target. The swing must start with a body pivot from the hips as the gun is mounted and it should continue on as butt and shoulder meet.

Here is another story of what the amount of forward allowance can mean to an individual. He was a young man who was normally a good shot but when he was confronted by high pheasants he very rarely hit them, and so his father sent him to a Shooting School. He had some shots at the walk-up and the driven partridges and did well, and the instructor wondered what the youngster's trouble was, until they reached the high tower. By then about half of the 150 cartridges allotted to the lesson had been used and the pupil fired off the last 75 at the high clays and never hit one of them. The instructor was fed up with telling the young man he was missing behind and finally he said : "You are wasting my time and your father's money but if you promise to do what I tell you I'll fetch another 50 cartridges and we'll try again."

When they started again the young fellow had decided that the instructor was talking nonsense and that most of the misses had been in front. He had promised, however, to do what he was told and he did not want any complaints to go back to his father, so in desperation he thought: 'I'll show this old blighter, I'll shoot yards and yards in front of the next target.'

Out came the clay, he fired and it was smashed. 'That couldn't be me,' he thought, and turned round to see if some-one else had shot it.

"No", said the instructor. "There is no one else with a gun here. You killed it yourself. Do you believe me now? Try some more like that."

They went through the rest of the cartridges and the pupil tried to maintain his 'impossible' lead, and sometimes he hit the clay and sometimes he missed. Another lesson was arranged for the next morning and he went home and slept on this new theory, and dreamed about it.

The next day he went out to the high tower again, listened to what the instructor had to say and started to shoot, full of determination to kill. He succeeded and broke eight clays out of ten. So home went a chastened young man who had made a big discovery. At the next pheasant shoot he shot several high birds and his father was so pleased that he wrote to congratulate the instructor on what had been achieved.

Do you believe that story? Oddly enough, it is entirely true.

In all but the most experienced sportsman there is a curious reluctance to shoot a considerable distance away from the target. If it is a going-away Down-The-Line clay, or a driven partridge flying over a hedge, this does not matter very much; quite a small lead will suffice. But on a long-range

[173]

shot, rocketing pheasants whether live or clay, it really is essential for all but the most exceptional man, with a very fast swing and a remarkably quick reaction, to shoot well in front. If you can make yourself do this you will have a very useful score at the high tower.

As a final inducement to persuade you to shoot ahead of a long range target consider the phenomenon known as shot stringing, which is the term used for describing how the pattern of shot has depth as well as breadth. When you look at the pellet marks on a pattern plate you may be tempted to visualise the shot in the air forming a similar flat pattern, whereas the charge actually spreads lengthways after it has left the gun, as well as sideways. The shot forms a column and at 40 yards the major part of it is in a cylinder about 8 feet long. This provides a margin of error, but only a small one, provided the shooter keeps ahead of his target. A 100% hit places the target in the middle of the 30-inch circle of shot pattern, although usually the target is only somewhere in the circle or even near the edge of it. If the leading edge of the circle is at the back of the target all but the odd stray pellet will miss it; if the circle is slightly ahead of the target the later pellets in the column of shot will meet the target as it moves forward and they may well be sufficient to register a kill. Therefore if the lead given to a crossing shot, and that includes vertical crossers as well as horizontal ones, is a little too long there is a good chance that the target will be hit because it will fly into a part of the pattern depth before the shot column has passed by. An error of too little lead can never put any of the pattern on the target.

'Before the shot column has passed by' was stated above, and this in fact is a very short time indeed, because the speed of the shot is much greater than the speed of the target. Shot stringing does, however, have the useful feature of making a

miss in front more difficult. If you overdo the forward allowance you may still have a kill; if you give insufficient lead you
never will.

Back to the Sporting Clays, and the next stand is pigeon.
It may be arranged in several different ways, one of which
is to have a bird crossing a gap between trees. This is good
practice because the shooter learns to ignore the trees which
at first can upset him considerably. When you try to shoot
real pigeon coming in to roost in a wood during March you
must never depend on finding a space between the branches
where you hope to kill your birds; if you do you will fire half
a dozen cartridges at about fifty possible targets. You should
ignore the trees altogether and imagine you are standing in
an open field; then you can shoot at any bird you see, swing
through and you will find that surprisingly few shots are in-
terrupted by the branches getting in the way.

On the clay pigeon layout the trap will be placed behind a
tree and you will face a gap of about 20 yards before another
tree blocks the view of the clay. This type of stand is better
in summer with full leaf on the trees than in winter when it
might still be possible to see the target through the bare
branches.

Shooting technique is normal for a crossing shot except
that you have to make yourself forget about the second
tree; as soon as the clay appears you mount your gun
and shoot and if the end of your swing leaves the barrels
pointing at the middle of the second tree, so much the better;
there will doubtless be a broken clay lying in the open space.
Unfortunately, it is all too easy to become anxious when you
are just leading past the target because you can see, out of the
corner of your eye, the tree which blocks the edge of the gap.
You cannot shoot through this tree, as you could through the
thin top branches of the bare March trees when you were

[175]

flighting real pigeon, but you can certainly catch the target before it goes behind the tree, if only you will imagine that there is no obstacle to a clear shot with a steady follow through. In the unlikely event of the organisers having made the gap sufficiently large for there to be time to take two shots you may keep the gun at your shoulder for the second shot, but you should double your lead.

The pigeon stand is more likely to include two birds, the general idea being that you are standing outside a wood and a pigeon flies out; when you fire at it the noise disturbs other birds which scatter in different directions. If the first bird comes out of a tree nearly above your head and goes straight away along the edge of the wood it presents the apparently downward moving target which you know from No. 1 High house at Skeet, and this is a popular arrangement on a Sporting layout.

We will assume that we have one going-away pigeon and one crosser, as in Figure VII. The second clay is released on the first shot. Adopt a normal stance and look over the muzzles to where you expect to pick up the first target which will be coming over your shoulder. When it appears follow the bird down through its flight line, keep the gun moving by bending from the waist and fire well below the target. This is similar to the Skeet shot but if the trap is up in a tree the clay will be higher and it may well be thrown from a strong trap, and so it will be faster and at a greater range than the Skeet bird. Do not underestimate the lead required as it is useless to shoot at the target; you must get down below it.

When the second pigeon flies out it goes across the field, and you should again take the butt off your shoulder and close the muzzles in behind the bird; there is no need to move your feet but your body should pivot round to allow you to swing out for the lead required by this crosser. You must be

[176]

careful not to lift your cheek off the stock while you are still taking the first shot, in anticipation of removing the butt from your shoulder. This point has been stressed before and it may be of interest to learn of the remark sometimes made to instructors at shooting schools: 'I know my cheek was on that time because I got a bang on the jaw.' This is a wildly mistaken reasoning because it shows that the cheek was *off* the stock, even if only a little way. If the cheek is locked solidly on the comb the shock of firing will scarcely be felt at all, and you will know from the feel of the swing where the shot has gone without needing to spoil everything by trying to have a look too soon.

Driven partridges can be thrown from a slightly raised trap behind a hedge or bush (Plate 48). They must be shot in front and as singles they are comparatively easy. They are not very high and a normal swing, firing as the gun passes the target, will suffice. In real life there would be a covey coming over but in clay competitions it is unusual to have more than pairs, although two traps can be arranged to throw four clays at a time. To shoot the pairs, concentrate on the first shot before you worry about the second and take the butt just off the shoulder between shots. The clays will probably be fairly close together and there is not a great deal of time to take the two shots, so the butt need only be lowered about three inches off the shoulder while the muzzles are moved across to follow in behind the second bird, when the gun is immediately re-mounted. If the clays come out of the trap one on each side of you it is best to shoot first whichever catches your eye, but if one comes overhead while the other goes out to a flank you would do better to take the overhead bird first because it will pass you sooner than the other and then it would be out of bounds. Do not allow the result of your first shot to affect the second, but try to keep to the steady

[177]

rhythm which is so essential when shooting pairs. (Plate 49.)

Natural teal have a reputation for climbing very fast and, indeed, the second barrel at teal, when they have accelerated into a nearly vertical lift, is one of the standard 'most difficult shots' about which shooting men like to argue. When disturbed teal can rise off water in a remarkable manner too, and the wildfowler needs to be quick and to shoot well above his bird if he is going to bring it to bag. The Springing Teal of the Sporting layout is a clay thrown from a trap at maximum elevation or mounted on its side if insufficient elevation is available; the strongest available trap is used so that the apex of the clay's flight is as high as possible. The correct place to kill this bird is on its way up, about 30 to 40 feet from the ground, but you may see people trying to catch it at the top of its flight as it stops momentarily before descending, and even trying to shoot it on the way down. Both these shots are more difficult to accomplish with consistent success that the correct method, but hits are sometimes achieved by what is little more than undeserved good luck. On a well-run shoot the rules will probably decree that the teal must be shot on the way up. (Plate 47.)

The trap will be fairly close to you, only about 10 or 15 yards away, and the initial speed of the clay is too great for you to be able to see it if you look at the traphouse. With the gun held in the normal position for preparation for the shot you should look about 15 feet up along the expected flight line; when you see the target mount the gun and swing it up quickly with the same bend back from the waist that you did at the high pheasants stand. Blot out the clay with the barrels and keep swinging a fraction of a second longer than you might think necessary before you fire. Hang onto the swing right up beyond the apex of the clay's flight and if it passes the barrels and comes into sight again you will know you

[178]

52. At the Shooting School a pair of clays are seen from the trap's position as they fly over the shooter, who is practising for "driven birds" in a Sporting competition.

53. This lad is having his first lesson and he cannot resist the temptation to lift his cheek off the stock as he fires. He wants to see the clay, which remains unbroken; in the photograph it is over the instructor's right shoulder.

54. Remember the trapper, who works unseen for many hours. This trap is loaded with a pair of clays.

55. "Bolting rabbits" are one of the targets in a Sporting layout, and the clays are flat, not dome shaped, and they have a broader edge on which to bowl along the ground.

56. This trap has a permanent base and protective screen, and it is used for pool shooting to amuse the members of a gun club while they are waiting their turns in the main event. The bar held by the trapper is for quick re-cocking of the trap.

57. It is warm work operating a trap in the summer. Here is a permanent trap installation with protective shield, and used for throwing "Driven grouse."

have not only given insufficient lead but also slowed up the swing too soon. Keep the weight forward and do not sway back onto your right leg.

The Rabbit is a special flat clay, not saucer-shaped like the flying variety, and with a wider edge to assist it to roll along the ground. The trap is fixed on its side, behind some cover, and it bowls the clay across an open grass space to another screen or bush on the far side of a gap of about 20 yards. (Plate 56). The important points to watch when shooting the rabbit are body movement and the amount of lead required.

Take up your position facing the place in the gap where you are going to make your kill and then pivot to the side until you are looking at the ground about 3 yards away from the screen concealing the trap. Now bend forward from the waist and line up the gun muzzles with that point on the ground where you are going to pick up the target. It is important to bend forward for this low shot, not stoop or crouch, because if you stand normally upright you will probably shoot over the top of the target. You should keep leaning forward as you swing into your shot, which will be taken with a good central stance and your left foot pointing in the 1 o'clock position; if you wrongly take up your initial stance towards the place where the rabbit first appears you will have to swing away from the central position and so be more likely to check the follow through. Scoring is 'kills to count' and so you are allowed a second barrel if necessary; in any case, with first or second barrel, keep the swing going right on through the screen at the side of the gap. If you hesitate about this you will probably miss, as with the pigeon that disappeared behind a tree.

Shooting rabbits is sometimes thought to be easy, whether they are clay or real, but this is not always so. The clay target moves fast and bounces along the ground and it needs an

[183]

appreciable forward allowance. You ought to be able to see the shot strike the ground and when you do, and the rabbit bolts off behind his cover, resolve to double the lead for the next shot. Not just, 'a bit more in front' but, 'I'm going to shoot twice as far ahead next time.'

That completes the list of targets normally found on Sporting layouts, and the inexperienced clay shooter may wonder how he is going to be able to practise these varied shots. Most gun clubs can arrange for some of the targets to be available but anyone entering seriously for a competition would be well advised to visit a Shooting School beforehand, and practise at some of the stands not often available at a club's grounds, such as Rocketing Pheasants or Bolting Rabbits. If you have no experience of this type of clay shooting you will probably want to have a look round the first layout you encounter before you attempt to shoot. But this is not a wise thing to do if you know the general form, because it can undermine confidence. If you go and watch a stand which you know you find difficult and you see someone shooting well you will doubtless go away feeling depressed; if you have a look at a stand where you know you ought to do well and you see a good shot missing you may think, 'Well, if he can't hit them they must be terribly difficult birds.' The result is that you return to start your round full of worry and wondering how you can possibly produce a good score. It is far better to go out and shoot regardless of what other people are doing or what their scores are, and to devote all your attention and concentration to killing the most important clay in the competition, which is the next one.

In a small club shoot, which is often promoted to help the club funds, it is reasonable to allow competitors to have a second or third attempt at a complete round. This will depend on the number of entries and the time available and it is not unusual to find a few keen competitors, who are in the running for the prizes, wanting to improve their scores. In a Championship meeting, however, only one entry is permitted and the choice of how early or late in the competition the shooting is done is, within certain limits, a matter of individual choice. For most people the choice is best made dependent only on outside commitments, which may be important in a two-day event; it is preferable to shoot when convenient and pay scant attention to other competitors' scores until the end, thus avoiding nervous anticipation.

Club layouts are often restricted by the space available, including the safety zone behind each stand. For this reason Skeet can be included in a club Sporting event, because Skeet targets bear a reasonable resemblance to many shots encountered in the field. A club competition can be made a little more 'sporting' than the more serious ones because it matters rather less who wins. Thus, the walk-up may be over rough country and the driven partridges may be sent over somewhat indiscriminately as 'coveys' of four birds. It would also be no bad idea on a club shoot to stop teal shooters trying to take the bird at the top of its flight or on the way down, by tying to wire between two trees on each side of the trap. The wire could have rags hung on it to the side of the actual flight line and the referee would call 'Lost' as soon as the clay passed the wire. A wildfowling club might have a trap on one side of a bank and arrange for the competitors to shoot from a kneeling position on the other side, because fowlers sometimes have to shoot in this way. Care must be taken, however, to ensure that such special types of shooting layouts do not develop into sources of danger. Club shoots often encourage novices by including a stand for instruction. (Plate 50.)

The light and the background affect the speed with which a clay target can be seen but as this is an acceptable hazard in normal shooting, difficult conditions must be expected in some parts of a Sporting layout. For instance, it is not possible to have all the stands facing north and therefore the competitors must be prepared for the extra handicap of shooting with the sun in their eyes, at least on one or two of the stands. It may be that this could influence the choice of which time of day is preferable for shooting one's round. Coloured clays were mentioned in the chapter on Olympic Trench as an assistance in seeing the target against a bad background; the colour dye is normally put only on the top of the clays, where it is visible on a receding and rising target, but it would be of no help on an overhead approaching clay.

Shooting a round on a fairly large Sporting layout where there are 100 targets may take about 150 cartridges, including some second barrel shots, and this could be tiring if one is not accustomed to it. The same applies to any major clay competition, whether Down-The-Line or Skeet, and it emphasises the need for practice beforehand. No one should suffer from a sore shoulder after shooting off a couple of hundred cartridges, because that could only be due to bad gun mounting or a badly fitting gun, both of which can be corrected; gun headache, however, is less easily cured and some shooters who are afflicted by it like to use the smaller cartridge with 1-oz. shot load. Should you be in this category you need not feel at a disadvantage on a Sporting layout; at the high tower, if it is in the 120 ft. class, the pattern may be a trifle thin at the edges but there are capable shots who manage very well, even at this stand, with the reduced shot load.

Sporting clays attract a greater variety of competitor than the more specialised events and this makes them more enjoyable and more open as far as the winner's identity is concerned. Down-The-Line experts and pigeon shooters, wildfowlers, rough shooters and game shots all have a chance and the interest is maintained when, for example, a popular fancy for the cup kills all the high pheasants and then misses half the driven grouse. This type of event is also good fun for the competitor who has no hope of winning any prize but who simply enjoys his shooting. To increase the interest there are often some special prizes as well as the Championship Cup; perhaps an award for the best performance at one particular stand, the high tower, for instance; and a Ladies' competition, and one for Father and Son; prizes for the best Veteran, Colt and Novice. Sporting Clays do not appear on the list of International competitions but they are shot on a National level. To many shooting men they represent the best and most interesting type of clay shooting; for the game shot they provide the only competition which includes driven birds.

CHAPTER NINE

THE CLAY SHOOTER'S YEAR

THE serious marksman must plan his year if he is going to make the best use of the time and money he has available.

Appendix 'B' shows a typical list of some of the major events held in the United Kingdom during the summer. There are also numerous smaller competitions organised by local clubs and these take place every week throughout the year; details are published in advance in *Shooting Times and Country Magazine*.

In Appendix 'B' one of the Championships is called "All Round" and this has not been mentioned before. It is an interesting competition as it generally includes several Sporting stands and also Skeet, Olympic Trench, Double-rise and Down-The-Line, probably 10 or 20 birds at each.

Specialists concentrate on one type of clay shooting and this may help them to reach success more quickly, but for a fuller enjoyment of the sport it is preferable to compete in all the different events, and to enter for the important ones with a high standard of shooting as well as the humbler meetings. A good shot is an all round shot; he may be only moderate at each type of shooting but he can hold his own anywhere and he enjoys it all. When preparing for a specific event he concentrates on it for a while, but it is the variety of shooting throughout the year which provides the most pleasure.

Small gun clubs can only afford to have a limited layout,

perhaps Down-The-Line and one trap hidden behind a hedge for driven birds. It should always be the aim of a club to provide easy shooting for beginners but also to have some difficult stands for the experienced shots. Initiative and ingenuity are needed if the club is to have such things as a trap fixed in a tree to throw high birds, and money is needed to pay for the traphouses of a Skeet layout and to keep the traps in good working order; but if the club is to prosper the members must be encouraged to try more difficult variations because it is the challenge in clay shooting which makes it interesting. The C.P.S.A. can help its individual members and also its affiliated clubs; some details are given in Appendix 'D'.

There are several gamekeepers' shoots each year, generally organised by a firm connected with shooting, and clay shoots are sometimes on the programme at fêtes and shows. One of the best of these is the Game Fair, held annually in a different part of the country. The important point is that more clay shooting goes on all the time than many people realise, and if you want to join in there is no lack of opportunity.

It is wise to book ahead for any important competition, both for entering and for accommodation if required. Hotels near the Game Fair, for instance, are booked up several months before the date. Entries for any competition are taken on the ground, but by posting your entry card in advance you will often save expense and you will sometimes be allotted an approximate time to shoot, which saves waiting around on the day and wasting time.

Sharing a car with other competitors can reduce the fairly high expenses, and if this seems obvious the reason for suggesting it is to indicate the difficulties which a solo clay shooter has to meet. It is practically essential to join a club, in order to practise shooting, certainly, but also to meet

[189]

others with whom plans can be made to assist each other when entering competitions.

All clay shoots provide a generous number of prizes. These include Challenge cups and replicas, cash, and such assorted items as cutlery, glass, gun cleaning kit, shooting stick, cartridge bag, tankard, clock and anything that the friends and sponsors of the competition can be persuaded to give. There are sometimes as many as five prizes in each shooting class. Cash prizes vary between about £15 and £5, but they are not likely to be large enough for anyone to make money out of his winnings. Winning a prize, irrespective of what it is, is helpful to a man's shooting because it makes him feel he must be some good; it satisfies his personal ambition and gives him confidence. In fact, his shooting may be better after winning third prize at an unimportant meeting, where the standard is fairly low, than after seeing his name at the bottom of the list at a Championship. On the practical side, many competitors might prefer £1 in cash, as a help towards their expenses, to a shooting stick or sherry decanter which they are unlikely to use; but, somewhat naturally, the firms who support the shoot usually prefer to give prizes in kind, from their own stock, rather than cash. (Plate 51.)

Clay shooting remains very much an amateur sport, in fact it is one of the few games which fully retain their amateur status. No one is paid to shoot and so far the semi-professional behaviour in other sports, whereby the top performers are paid to say they use certain equipment, has not made its appearance. Some cups are given for the best combined score at more than one event; for example, at a Skeet and a Sporting Championship or at Skeet, Sporting and Down-The-Line. Most of the main competitions also include a team event with a trophy for the winners.

Entrance fees are about £23 for a 100-bird Championship meeting, including 125 cartridges, or about £15 if cartridges are not included. Cartridges are always available at the meeting and sometimes a rule states that 'only cartridges purchased on the ground may be used.' One object of this rule is, quite fairly, to help the organisers to defray their expenses, which they do by buying cartridges at a reduced bulk rate and selling them at the standard price; another reason for the rule is to ensure equality among all competitors.

At a small club meeting the entrance fee may be as little as 75p for 25 birds and these are the competitions which the beginner should enter. With all the arrangements made for him he does not have to pay much more than the cost of his cartridges and he has quite a good chance of winning a prize, perhaps in the Novice or Non-expert class.

Pool shooting is often included as a sideline and it may be 5 or 10 birds Down-The-Line. The pool is made up of the entrance fees, and winnings are paid out every hour or so. Anyone can go along while waiting for his turn in the main competition, pay 25p for 5 birds, or perhaps a little more, and have some practice which may be financially rewarding. A percentage of the pool is retained to pay for the staff to run it and for the clays. This sort of shooting should be taken light-heartedly and if you just 'have a go' for the fun of it you may surprise yourself by making an excellent score.

You cannot make money at clay shooting, as you can if you play sufficiently good golf or bridge, and the poor man is at a disadvantage when compared with the rich man. To reach the top a great deal of practice is necessary and this requires time and money. You can, however, enjoy your shooting on a more modest budget if you enter for the smaller club shoots.

Badges are awarded by the C.P.S.A., on application from the secretary of an affiliated gun club, for shooting '25

Straight' or '50 Straight' or '100 Straight' in club shoots. They are also given to Class winners of major events, including Sporting. Shotgunners, like rifle marksmen, often wear their badges on the backs of their jackets where they can be seen while their owners are in action.

Towards the end of a shoot there are nearly always several competitors with the same scores, and various methods are used to sort out the final results. For instance, in a Sporting event those who have tied for a place might be required in the shoot-off to take five pairs from the high tower; at Skeet or Down-The-Line they would shoot another 25 bird series. Sometimes there are still equal scores even after this extra shooting and so then 'Miss and Out' may be applied; this means that the rivals shoot alternatively and the first one to miss drops out. In less important competitions this procedure may be adopted in the first place, in order to save time when the company is becoming impatient for the prize-giving and wants to start for home. Where there are cash prizes it may be decided to 'Add and Divide'; if two competitors tie for first place the prize money for first and second is added together and the two then receive half the total each.

'Add and Divide' and 'Miss and Out' can normally be adopted only if the contestants agree, or if it is specified in the programme. If it is not in the programme and if one disagrees the proper shoot-off of 10 or 25 birds must be carried out. This is really fairer but it can be a somewhat tedious business.

Ambitions to win prizes should be coupled with the aim of a place in the club team, followed by aspirations for the county team and then to represent one's country. Clay shooting is primarily a recreation but you will improve quicker if you set yourself a task to achieve, a standard to reach, even an individual to beat in competition. A keen youngster once entered for his first Sporting Shoot, and he was fascinated by the skill of the man who was shooting before him. He followed this crack shot round the course and eventually he plucked up courage to speak to the unknown master.

"Congratulations," he said. "I wish I could shoot like that!"

Back came the curt reply, "I dare say you do."

This upset the young man at first, and perhaps that was the intention. But as the words rankled in his mind he determined to return their meaning in full to the speaker. He practised diligently throughout the year and when that meeting came round again he went in and won it.

A fighting spirit and a will to win is needed for success. When you plan your shooting year set your sights on a definite objective and go all out to achieve it.

How can you become a better shot? The answer can only be 'by practising' and that includes dry practice and exercises to improve the co-ordination of the movements required in gun mounting. You must practise correctly and you should physically do what is recommended in this book for all the various types of shot. If you only read about how to shoot 'No. 1 High house' at Skeet you will forget when you come to try it, unless you have previously tried out the various actions slowly, using an unloaded gun. Dry practice can help enormously, if you will be bothered to do it. A beginner should go through the shooting instruction in Chapters 4, 5, and 8 at his club's grounds, but only after he has experienced the feel of each shot with the book in front of him and a gun in his hands. An experienced shot who wants to improve should study the instruction, decide where he may be going wrong and then carry out the drill advocated, first with an empty gun and then by doing some practise shooting.

All shooters need practice in order to improve and to keep

in tune with their guns. Here are some exercises which can be done at any time in or near your home.

1. Handle your gun as often as possible. Keep it assembled in a cupboard rather than dismantled in a case. Pick it up and mount it at any object you can see through the window, having made sure that it is unloaded.

2. Walk about outside and put the gun muzzles on some object, a stone, a tin or anything that catches your eye. With the butt still down, get your stance right, weight on left foot and see if you can mount the butt to your shoulder without the muzzle leaving the target.

3. Learn to acquire a good grip on the gun with your right hand. A slack grip means that the butt is not properly into the shoulder and the whole stock can slip back through your hand on recoil; this causes the trigger guard to bruise your second finger, the muzzles to wander off the target as you pull the trigger and the comb to jump, perhaps banging you on the jaw. To practise this grip mount the gun at some mark slightly above the horizontal. Take away your left hand and hold the muzzles on the mark. This shows how the grip of your right hand must be firmly locked onto the small of the butt, and how it also holds the butt well into your shoulder, which should be bearing forward against the butt. Do this several times and check that you have taken a firm hold with your right hand and placed the butt correctly into your shoulder; if you have not done so it will be apparent when you take your left hand off the barrels.

4. To check that you can make a good point at a stationary object, mount the gun at your eye in a mirror.

[194]

You will be able to see if the barrels are pointing askew and you can also check that your eye is in the right place in relation to the rib, as shown in Plate 10. Always remember that your shoulder must follow into the butt, which should not be pulled back against your shoulder.

5. Outside in the garden again, or at the club's shooting grounds, try pointing at more stationary targets with an unloaded gun, but include some body pivoting. Choose a mark in front of you and one each side at about a right angle from your front. Bring the gun up at each mark in turn, pivoting the body round so that your chest remains obliquely to the direction in which the gun points. Do not let your arms swing across your body, keep leaning forward, weight on your left foot and right heel clear of the ground. The heel should swing to right and left as your body pivots and when you have the gun well round to the left your right heel ought to be almost as far off the ground as is a golfer's at the end of a drive. Keep your left leg stiff and the rest of your body supple. Swing slowly at first and then speed up the gun mounting, and beware of dropping your weight back onto your right foot when you point to the mark on the right-hand side. Study Plates 11, 12, 13, 14.

6. Equip yourself with some snap caps, which allow the triggers of an unloaded gun to be pulled without endangering the strikers. Go out into the country and practise some swinging. Put the muzzles on a starling or any other bird that appears and swing out in front of it and say 'Bang!' to yourself when you would have fired or, if you have snap caps, pull the triggers on these practice shots. Try to note where the gun is pointing

as you 'fire', but do not check the swing and do not look specifically at the barrels. Find some telegraph wires or overhead electric cables and take up your stance in front of them; put the muzzles on a wire while your body pivots and carries them along, and see that the muzzles remain on the line while the gun is being mounted, so that they never deviate from the line until well after the shot would have been taken. The sequence of action is:

1. Body starts *first* to move along the line on which you are going to shoot.
2. Left hand connects the muzzles to the line.
3. Left hand holds the muzzles securely on the line while the body continues to pivot and the butt is raised to meet the shoulder. When you can do this drill accurately you will feel certain, as you pull the trigger, that you are right on the target and that had it been a real bird you would surely have killed it. In order to keep the muzzle on the line your eye is following you must lean forward directly over your left hip and pivot easily on it. To help this, cultivate a feeling of reaching out, pushing the muzzles forward and up, but with your body and not your arms. Keep the body pushed forward with the toes of your right foot.
4. Even if you confine your shooting to clays you still need to practise the overhead shot, at Sporting 'High Pheasants' or at Skeet No. 8 stand. Try that position in Plate 29. Reach forward with a gun, think to yourself 'Up!' and try to put the gun as near as possible to your imaginary target. Keep the left foot firm and allow the right heel to rise. Swing to the perpendicular and a little beyond, but remind yourself that you actually took the shot a little before the gun became verti-

[196]

cal. Tell yourself that you must not lean back onto the right foot, for that would mean pulling the muzzles back, down away from your target and you are trying to reach up, and up, as far as you can. Do this exercise until you have the feel of the sway forward and until you are confident that you have lost any tendency to want to drop back onto your right foot.

When you plan your shooting year remember that everyone needs to keep in practice. As well as doing practice for its own sake, and exercise to train the body, you need real shooting practice before any competition. This will speed up your reactions and help you to see the clays earlier in their flight. A quick pick up of the target is axiomatic of first class shooting and few mediocre performers realise that their betters have practically completed their shots before they themselves have observed which way the clay is going. You can speed up your technique by watching the clays leave the trap when you are not shooting. Strive to see them earlier and earlier, and the instant that your eye picks one up glance quickly out along its expected course; look ahead of it and note whether it flies as you have predicted or whether your estimation is at fault. By such concentrated observation you can teach yourself to see clays quickly, and instantly to judge their flight line.

The clay shooter's year can be a full one and it is certain to be rewarding if he will remember that the main object is the enjoyment of overcoming even a modest challenge. Most of us can never become super shots, and many cannot afford to shoot sufficiently often even to reach their best standard. No one should be disheartened if his performance is insufficient to win a big competition because there are thousands like him, enjoying their sport and shooting for fun.

CHAPTER TEN

SHOOTING FOR FUN

NEARLY all boys like guns and if they own one, even a toy, at an early age they should be taught the fundamental rules of safety. Graduating from air-gun and .410 to a 12-bore the youngster wants to shoot game and vermin but this is not so easily arranged now-a-days for the town dweller. Shooting, like fishing, is a perpetual challenge and there is always something new to learn about it. Once interested in it, the desire to continue shooting lasts a lifetime and this is where the clay bird offers so much.

Any parent who wishes to help his son to learn to handle a shotgun should have no difficulty in finding a gun club somewhere nearby, and with a little encouragement and financial aid the boy will soon be shooting well. An older man, perhaps remembering the fun he had with a gun when he was a boy, may want to take up shooting again and he too should join his local club. Appendix 'A' lists organisations which can advise about the localities of some 300 or more gun clubs throughout the British Isles.

The experienced clay shooter is aware of these facts but he may still wonder if he can get more out of his sport. He can do so if he will avoid an attitude of intense seriousness, although concentration is necessary while actually shooting, and if he will help newcomers to learn as much as possible about all aspects of the game. No keen shot ever regrets the

58.
A light trap simply installed on a box and held down by angle irons. This would be suitable for use by a few friends who had the loan of a field where they could put in some practice at short notice.

59. A fully mobile trap. The operator has a seat and he fires the self-cocking trap by pushing out with his left foot. The small handle by his right hand alters the elevation of the trap. No fixing in the ground is required and the whole thing is easily carried in a car boot.

60. A trap simply arranged by bolting it to a wooden plank, prevented from jumping forward by an angle iron in the ground. Straw bales behind the trapper protect him from the guns who will be out of the picture, to the right.

61. Ladies also shoot clays and here is a good position by a Skeet shooter, albeit she is using rather a handful of an automatic.

time and money expended on overcoming difficulties in order
to reach success, least of all that spent on going to a Shooting
School for lessons from a professional coach. If the fees seem
high it should be remembered that most of them are made up
of the cost of cartridges and clays, and the actual teaching
is extremely good value for money. The instructor can see
the shot in the air and he can nearly always spot his pupil's
mistakes in the first five minutes of shooting. (Plates 52 and
53).

The Captain of the team which had won an International
Match was once heard to say in his speech following the cele-
bration dinner : "I've always been ambitious about my shooting but I did it mainly because I enjoyed it. I was lucky in
the help I received from my parents and friends, but to reach
this position I am in today has cost me a lot of money over
the years. I would just like to say that I wouldn't want any
of it back. I've enjoyed every minute, and every penny has
been worth while." The same sentiments apply to hun-
dreds of clay shooters at more humble levels of achievement.

You may wonder how you can shoot competitively and
still have a job. The answer is that most competitions take
place on Saturdays and in the evenings during the summer.
But careful planning is needed if you have to take days off
work to travel further afield than the local shoots.

Temperament plays an important part in all shooting, especially when the stakes are high and critical spectators are
at hand. This is an individual matter and some people are
affected more than others. If you are nervous when performing in public you must try to train yourself to be natural,
to be simply the one who shoots because he likes it. This
may be more easily said than done but it is possible, with self-
discipline. If you think 'I *must* get this next target,' you will

probably miss it, because you are trying too hard. Instead, say to yourself : 'I'm here to enjoy myself, not to worry about scores.' Make sure that your stance is right, and that the gun is mounted correctly, and the butt locked against your cheek and shoulder. Concentrate on your shooting, do not be careless but relax and think, 'Here goes, I'm going to kill this bird.'

This should remove the nervous tension and as the anxiety disappears you can be your normal self, free and easy, a trained shooter doing what he likes to do. If you can do this your scores will quickly mount up, and you may even wonder why! The ease with which a nervous performer can fail to give of his best is the reason why so much stress is put on the idea that clay shooting is for fun.

Lack of confidence causes poor shooting but it can be regained after a success, however modest. Do not, therefore, aim too high at first. Enter competitions which are a challenge but not those in a class far above your own. Remember that you may be allowed to 'shoot for birds only' if you want shooting experience without the harrowing thought of seeing your score to be about half that of anyone else. Confidence makes the clays look big and slow, unlike the small, fast ones that the anxious man sees.

Too much confidence may also invite failure, as happened to a visitor to a Shooting School who wanted some practice before going in for a Sporting Clays competition. He had not done much walking-up and had never been in a grouse butt, and so he concentrated on these stands, and just had a few shots at the high pheasants and the pigeon at which he was very good. When he shot in the competition he started well on the walk-up and then did excellently at the driven grouse; at the pigeon stand things started to go wrong and when he came to the pheasants he missed them all! Here was a bad case of too much confidence, followed immediately by trying too hard as soon as trouble appeared.

When you have entered for a competition do not let the fact prey on your mind beforehand. Think only that you have an interesting day in front of you, when you are going to meet a friendly crowd and have some good shooting at whatever the organisers have arranged. Of course you will miss some of the clays, everybody does; if you never missed the target the challenge would not exist and the whole business would be too dull to be worth doing. If you are really quite a bad shot comfort yourself with the thought that you have more enjoyment than the good shots, because it is more of a pleasant surprise when you do hit the target! You also have more scope for improvement and more achievements waiting for you.

Still on the theme of being your natural self when shooting, do not alter your normal behaviour beforehand. Do not, for instance, give up tobacco and liquor the day before because that will certainly upset your nerves. And if you go to bed early with the intention of having a good night's sleep the chances are that you will wake several hours before it is time to get up, and lie in bed worrying about the ordeal to come.

Unlike game, clays have no close season, and as well as providing a source of competition they can help the ordinary shooter to keep in practice between the game seasons. Many of the clients of Shooting Schools are game and clay shots whose normal shooting companions would consider them as being beyond the need for lessons; they are the good shots whose performance is always admired, but they know the need to keep in practice and to check any faults that may develop before these turn into bad habits.

The shooting instruction in this book is based on these

facts: with a correct stance, the weight forward, the body pivoting from the waist and the gun muzzles held between eye and target from the moment the latter is seen until the shot is fired, the gun must be moving exactly on the same course as the target. The extra requirement to hit a moving target is forward allowance, which the shooter learns to judge by experience, bearing in mind that it is virtually impossible to miss in front. The body movements are co-ordinated by the brain and when they are working correctly the result is like a machine in the constant repetition of the same actions. Shooting '100 straight' for instance, must be machine-like in its consistent accuracy. Nevertheless, the machine sometimes goes wrong; then the game shot or the competitive clay shooter who begins missing birds he knows he ought to kill can regain his form by analysing his actions and finding where the fault starts. Self-analysis is not easy, but spotting shooting faults is quite simple to a shooting coach. Practise your gun mounting because once that is right you will find that hitting the target is not difficult.

Do not be dismayed at the idea of having to buy several guns to shoot clays; there are lucky fellows who own a gun for Skeet and another for Down-The-Line, and also a game gun for Sporting shoots, but you can do very well with one standard gun. You will become accustomed to the feel of it, the balance and trigger pulls until it becomes almost a part of you.

An old gentleman, well known at many famous covert shoots, remarked when he retired from active shooting at the age of 76, "Talking of guns, d'you know I think I've had more pleasure out of that old gun of mine than many of my friends with their expensive ones." The gun he spoke of was a double-barrelled 12-bore and it had been given to him on his 21st birthday; it cost £4 15s. new. He was a very good shot and could have as much shooting as he liked. He used to travel round in a Rolls Royce and when his old, cheap gun was taken from its case there were some surprised expressions on the faces of those watching. He put as many birds in the bag as anyone, which certainly shows that it is the man behind the gun who matters and not the weapon he uses, whether he shoots pheasants or clays. This old sportsman was exceptional, and most of us would do better to buy the best gun we can afford. Do not, however, be depressed if you own only a modest old gun; as long as it suits you and fits you it will kill a lot of clay birds for you at every type of event.

You should know something about clay traps, of which there are several varieties. Pamphlets on traps are mentioned in Appendix 'D'; they describe some of the traps available on the U.K. market. If you can find a location suitable for clay shooting a cheap way of having some practice is to buy a Hand Flinger, which is a kind of sling for throwing clays. Light traps can be fixed on a wooden box, as in Plate 58. A heavier trap needs a permanent base, as in Plate 56, or it can be temporarily screwed to a heavy piece of timber such as a railway sleeper, as in Plate 60. The pamphlet 'How to Run Small Shoots' in Appendix 'D' describe how to instal traps.

A trap for use by a few friends who want to shoot together occasionally should be easily set up, and a good one which needs no securing to a base is shown in Plate 59.

A recent arrival on the market is a Mini-trap, which is held in the hands, and which throws 'mini' clays; these are both smaller and cheaper than the standard ones.

As a general rule a trap which operates by the spring contracting is more reliable than one in which the spring expands to provide the propelling force, and it has a smoother action.

All traps must have a shot-proof screen round them and the commonly used straw bales may not be sufficient by themselves, especially if they are carelessly assembled; sheets of corrugated iron ought to be placed inside the barrier of straw bales.

Traps can be dangerous and a loaded one gives no indication to the inexperienced eye as to where its arm moves when it is fired. Anyone who is going to operate a trap, or even examine it, should have the danger area of the throwing arm explained to him. Even experienced trappers may become careless about safety precautions, perhaps with fatal results.

There was once a fairly big shoot arranged where the organisers did not realise how long it took to instal the traps. The job was left until the morning of the shoot and was entrusted to a couple of mechanics from the local garage. Time was running out, with early competitors arriving and the traps still not ready. A competitor who had experience with traps saw one of the mechanics sitting on the ground in front of an automatic trap, doing some adjustments with his face a few inches from the throwing arm. The trap was cocked and the pulling lever was in position. A child or even a dog might have moved the pulling lever and released the trap.

When he saw this incredibly dangerous situation the competitor pointed it out to the mechanic who, being in a hurry, said he knew what he was doing, did not like interference and wished people would mind their own business. He was left alone.

Shortly afterwards the trap did go off and slashed the man across the forehead. He was rushed to hospital, where he died.

Traps may cost anything from £10 to about £2,000 or £3,000 for the most elaborate fully automatic electric types;

these expensive ones can earn their keep, however, by saving trappers' wages at a busy club.

Remember the trapper, an important person who is rarely seen and is not always paid very much. At small shoots he may not be paid at all, being a volunteer for a strenuous and not particularly pleasant job. If there is a collection taken for the trappers be generous in your contribution. Plates 54 and 57 show a couple of hard-working trappers who would doubtless be grateful if someone sent them over a glass of beer during a lull in the proceedings.

The need for safety precautions can never be overstressed and so you are reminded again that nearly all accidents occur with guns which are supposedly unloaded. It is essential to check that your gun is unloaded whenever you leave the firing line, and when you put it into a car or bring it into a building. Experience at some club shoots shows that many people are appallingly casual about their safety drill, and instructors at Shooting Schools are constantly seeing experienced shots forget elementary safety precautions; for instance, a client will load two cartridges, fire one and then start to walk to another stand with a live cartridge still in the gun. Details are given in Appendix 'D' of two pamphlets, 'The Gun Code' and 'Safe Gun Handling' which should be read by everyone who owns a gun.

Anyone can enjoy clay shooting, irrespective of age or sex. Many ladies are extremely good shots and their only handicap might be the difficulty of wielding a heavy gun. A 16-bore game gun or under-and-over is usually more suitable than a heavy repeater. (See Plate 61). Left-handers are also more numerous than may be supposed, despite the fact that a person who is normally left-handed often has a right master eye; in this case he might be better advised to learn to shoot from his right shoulder.

Clay pigeon shooting is an excellent outdoor recreation which provides an answer to the desires of many people, particularly city dwellers. It is a challenge, a chance to do something different from one's normal life, an opportunity to meet good company and a competitive sport which brings few material gains but much of the intangible satisfaction of personal achievement. Keep those muzzles swinging and you will surely find your reward.

SHOOTING ORGANISATIONS

1. The Clay Pigeon Shooting Association. Director's address: 107 Epping New Road, Buckhurst Hill, Essex. About 400 affiliated clubs.

2. Scottish Clay Pigeon Association. Secretary's address: 42 Hill Street, Tillicoultry, Clackmannanshire. 80 affiliated clubs.

3. Welsh Clay Pigeon Shooting Association. Secretary's address: Trefrane, Roch, Haverfordwest, Dyfed. About 20 affiliated clubs.

4. Ulster Clay Pigeon Shooting Association. Secretary's address: 6 Springhill Avenue, Bangor, Co. Down. 11 affiliated clubs.

5. Irish Clay Pigeon Association. Secretary's address: 20 Butterfield Drive, Rathfarnham, Dublin 14, Eire.

6. The British Association for Shooting and Conservation. Director's address: Marford Mill, Rossett, Clwyd, Wales. 240 affiliated organisations, most of which are primarily interested in wildfowling but many are concerned with rough shooting and clay pigeon.

TYPICAL PROGRAMME
OF MAIN EVENTS

APRIL
>   English Open Sporting Championship.
>   British Open Sporting Championship.

MAY
>   Welsh Open Down-The-Line Championship.
>   British Open Continental Skeet.
>   Scottish Grand Final.

JUNE
>   English Open Down-The-Line Championship.
>   International Down-The-Line Tournament.

JULY
>   Welsh Open Grand Prix (Olympic Trench).
>   English Open Grand Prix (Olympic Trench).
>   Grand Prix of Great Britain (Olympic Trench).
>   British Open Double-rise Championship.
>   Game Fair.

AUGUST
>   British Open Skeet Championship.
>   English Open Single-barrel and Double-rise Championships.
>   English Open Skeet Championship.

SEPTEMBER
>   English Open Handicap-by-distance Championship.
>   English Open All-round Championship.

In addition local gun clubs run shoots every week throughout the year. Details in *Shooting Times and Country Magazine*.

RECORD AND CHAMPIONSHIP WINNERS

1. Record runs for breaking clays are usually recognised only when they occur at one meeting. The total, therefore, cannot exceed that of the number of birds offered to the competitors. But scores are sometimes added together from one meeting to another, giving figures like those of Fred Etchen (U.S.A.) who broke 472 clays without a miss in the 1920's. American records also show a run of 565 consecutively broken clays as long ago as 1909 by C. G. Spencer.

2. The world record for Skeet, recognised by the International Shooting Union, goes to N. Durnev (U.S.S.R.) with 200 kills from 200 birds in October 1962.

3. An Olympic Trench record, not officially recognised, was made by J. Wheater who broke 199/200 clays in Germany in 1961.

4. Two English records are:
   Down-The-Line—J. Wheater, 200/200 kills on 29th and 30th May 1959.
   Skeet—J. Wheater, 100/100 kills on 14th June 1958.

5. A record which has caught the interest of several good shots is the time taken to break 1,000 clays. J. Wheater, in September 1957, took 42 minutes $22\frac{1}{2}$ seconds to do this, and went on shooting for the full hour to kill a total of 1,308 birds.

6. Recent Championship winners in England are:
   (a) English Open Down-The-Line (100 birds).
      1961—H. Baxter, 200/200 points.
      1962—B. W. Bailey, 200/200 points.
      1963—J. H. Sheffield, 196/200 points.
      1964—M. H. Wootton, 196/200 points.

1965—J. H. Tinkler, 193/200 points.
1966—E. A. Grantham, 198/200 points.
1967—W. Heald, 299/300 points.
1968—B. W. Bailey, 296/300 points.
1969—J. W. Cook, 295/300 points.
1970—B. W. Bailey, 298/300 points.
1971—M. N. Jenkins, 298/300 points.
1972—G. J. Braddick, 297/300 points.
1973—B. L. Bradley 297/300 points.
1974—W. J. Joyce, 299/300 points.
1975—G. Brocklesby, 300/300 points.
1976—K. R. Borley, 300/300 points.
1977—K. Bond, 299/300 points.
1978—C. A. Stewart, 298/300 points.
1979—P. Harness, 299/300 points.
1980—M. C. Robson, 298/300 points.
1981—K. J. Hicks, 297/300 points.

(b) British Open Down-The-Line (100 birds).
1961—F. B. Edwards (Ireland), 293/300 points.
1962—R. D. Browning, 296/300 points.
1963—R. Flynn (Ireland), 292/300 points.
1964—J. W. Cook (England), 298/300 points.
1965—C. A. J. Pickard (England), 298/300 points.
1966—A. Poskitt (England), 297/300 points.
1967—W. Heald (England), 298/300 points.
1968—A. Poskitt (England), 297/300 points.
1969—T. S. Brockie (Scotland), 287/300 points.
1970—A. Poskitt (England), 298/300 points.
1971—B. W. Bailey, 297/300 points.
1972—A. Poskitt, 298/300 points.
1973—R. H. Carter, 298/300 points.
1974—G. Lewis, 300/300 points.

1975—P. Woodward, 295/300 points.
1976—M. Campbell, 295/300 points.
1977—E. Wilson, 297/300 points.
1978—M. C. Robson, 296/300 points.
1979—R. Carter, 299/300 points.
1980—A. A. Bell, 299/300 points.
1981—H. Mattocks, 298/300 points.

(c) English Open Sporting (80 birds).
1961—E. T. Peacock, 75/80.
1962—H. A. Simpson, 73/80.
1963—R. Townroe, 74/80.
1964—J. Collins, 73/80.
1965—A. Bonnett, 78/80.
1966—J. Barton, 74/80.
1967—R. G. Carter, 76/80.
1968—R. G. Carter, 75/80.
1969—W. Sykes, 76/80.
1970—D. Carpenter, 75/80.
1971—K. A. Broomfield 88/100.
1972—P. R. Howe, 89/100.
1973—R. H. Copplestone, 89/100.
1974—S. L. Cooper, 92/100.
1975—A. Secker, 78/86.
1976—R. C. Ireland, 88/100.
1977—P. R. Howe, 94/100.
1978—W. J. Sykes, 90/100.
1979—B. J. Wells, 88/100.
1980—G. Stirzaker, 89/100.
1981—D. J. Lawton, 88/100.

(d) British Open Sporting (100 birds).
1961—J. Wheater, 91/100.

[213]

1962—J. Wheater, 89/100.
1963—S. Gulyas, 84/100.
1964—J. Wheater, 86/100.
1965—D. D. Dodd, 85/100.
1966—R. G. Carter, 87/100.
1967—A. Bonnett, 92/100.
1968—R. J. Simpson, 90/100.
1969—W. J. Sykes, 87/100.
1970—K. A. Broomfield, 90/100.
1971—J. Wheater, 97/100.
1972—J. Wheater, 91/100.
1973—B. J. Wells, 92/100.
1974—M. Emms, 89/100.
1975—P. R. Howe, 91/100.
1976—P. R. Howe, 90/100.
1977—J. H. Ling, 84/100.
1978—J. I. Stafford, 88/100.
1979—A. B. Hebditch, 92/100.
1980—J. Welham, 92/100.
1981—B. Frost, 92/100.

(e) English Open Skeet (100 birds).
1961—J. R. Matthews, 94/100.
1962—J. P. Breckon, 96/100.
1963—J. H. Sheffield, 97/100.
1964—C. Wirnhier, 186/200.
1965—N. E. Sansome, 98/100.
1966—C. J. Sephton, 96/100.
1967—E. A. Grantham, 92/100.
1968—E. A. Grantham, 96/100.
1969—D. Seabrook, 97/100.
1970—D. N. Dixon, 73/75.
1971—D. Seabrook, 100/100.

1972—W. J. Sykes, 98/100.
1973—D. D. Dodd, 100/100.
1974—J. H. Sheffield, 100/100.
1975—J. H. Sheffield, 100/100.
1976—J. H. Sheffield, 99/100.
1977—E. Chapman, 99/100.
1978—A. G. Parr, 99/100.
1979—P. Billington, 99/100.
1980—I. MacDonald, 100/100.
1981—I. Payne, 100/100.

(f) British Open Skeet (100 birds).
1961—J. S. Edgar, 97/100.
1962—A. J. Steele, 95/100.
1963—N. E. Sansome, 97/100.
1964—R. Townroe, 97/100.
1965—N. E. Sansome, 94/100.
1966—R. Townroe, 92/100.
1967—N. E. Sansome, 93/100.
1968—B. A. Smith, 98/100.
1969—J. R. Matthews, 99/100.
1970—D. J. Styles, 99/100.
1971—D. Seabrook, 98/100.
1972—D. Tilden, 97/100.
1973—T. Poskitt, 100/100.
1974—W. J. Sykes, 99/100.
1975—B. J. Wells, 99/100.
1976—D. Ellis, 100/100.
1977—G. Paget, 100/100.
1978—J. Welham, 100/100.
1979—J. M. Brazzell, 100/100.
1980—H. Harup, 99/100.
1981—B. Parker, 100/100.

(g) English Open Grand Prix, Olympic Trench (100 birds).

1961—V. B. Huthart, 97/100.
1962—J. Wheater, 98/100.
1963—E. Fear, 91/100.
1964—J. R. Braithwaite, 94/100.
1965—J. R. Braithwaite, 94/100.
1966—J. Wheater, 96/100.
1967—E. A. Grantham, 96/100.
1968—G. A. Freeman, 96/100.
1969—B. W. Bailey, 97/100.
1970—B. W. Bailey, 193/200.
1971—R. G. Carter, 193/200.
1972—B. W. Bailey, 200/200 points.
1973—J. Tennison, 191/200.
1974—J. Tennison, 191/200.
1975—D. J. Calvert, 193/200.
1976—Ron Carter, 184/200.
1977—J. A. Brown, 192/200.
1978—K. R. Wilson, 186/200.
1979—P. Boden, 184/200.
1980—P. Boden, 189/200.
1981—J. Tennison, 196/200.

(h) British Open Grand Prix, Olympic Trench (200 birds).

1961—E. Fear, 192/200.
1962—J. Y. Stewart, 193/200.
1963—F. J. Eisenlauer (U.S.A.), 191/200.
1964—J. Wheater, 190/200.
1965—J. R. Braithwaite, 179/200.
1966—J. R. Braithwaite, 275/300 birds.
1967—J. R. Braithwaite, 188/200.

1968—J. R. Braithwaite, 188/200.
1969—J. Wheater, 187/200.
1970—J. R. Braithwaite, 194/200.
1971—B. W. Bailey, 195/200.
1972—B. W. Bailey, 189/200.
1973—S. Basagani, 190/200.
1974—B. W. Bailey, 193/200.
1975—P. Boden, 192/200.
1976—J. Tennison, 193/200.
1977—E. Azkue, 190/200.
1978—P. Croft, 190/200.
1979—J. Tennison, 194/200.
1980—P. Boden, 195/200.
1981—B. Van Limbeek, 191/200.

(i) British Open Grand Prix, International Skeet (200 birds).
1967—A. Bonnett, 190/200.
1968—J. F. Pennington, 188/200.
1969—J. M. Neville, 186/200.
1970—R. W. Leach, 191/200.
1971—J. M. Neville, 192/200.
1972—C. J. Sephton, 192/200.
1973—J. M. Neville, 194/200.
1974—A. B. Hebditch, 194/200.
1975—W. J. Sykes, 196/200.
1976—B. J. Wells, 197/200.
1977—B. J. Simpson, 195/200.
1978—P. Bentley, 194/200.
1979—M. Billington, 194/200.
1980—P. Bentley, 196/200.
1981—J. Woolley, 193/200.

(j) English Open Grand Prix, International Skeet (200 birds).

1967—A. Bonnett, 173/200.
1968—C. J. Sephton, 187/200.
1969—M. Michaelides, 188/200.
1970—B. A. Smith, 190/200.
1971—C. J. Sephton, 193/200.
1972—J. M. Neville, 198/200.
1973—A. Bonnett, 193/200.
1974—T. Poskitt, 193/200.
1975—J. M. Neville, 199/200.
1976—T. Poskitt, 190/200.
1977—J. M. Neville, 188/200.
1978—J. M. Neville, 198/200.
1979—J. M. Neville, 193/200.
1980—B. Rossetti, 197/200.
1981—W. J. Sykes, 196/200.

7. Percy Stanbury's shooting successes include:
   (a) English International team, 26 times.
   (b) British Skeet Champion, 5 times.
   (c) British Sporting Champion, 5 times.
   (d) English Down-The-Line Champion, 7 times.
   (e) British Down-The-Line Champion, 4 times.
   (f) High Gun at International meetings, 4 times.

SOURCES OF INFORMATION
ON CLAY SHOOTING

1. 'Regulations for Clay Pigeon Shooting'. Published by the International Shooting Union in Wiesbaden-Klarenthal, West Germany. Available from the C.P.S.A.
2. 'Regulations for Skeet'. The I.S.U. rules with C.P.S.A. amendments. Available from the C.P.S.A.
3. 'Rules and Regulations for Down-The-Line Shooting'. Issued by the C.P.S.A.
4. 'Clay Pigeon Shooting Clubs'. Describes how-to form a club, how to arrange meetings, make rules, and what to do to ensure that the club prospers. Available from C.P.S.A.
5. 'Area and County Championships'. Rules for organising these local events. Available from the C.P.S.A.
6. 'How to run small shoots'. Describes how to organise a clay shoot at a fête, show or fair; includes notes on equipment, layout, safety, unusual types of shooting, prizes, obtaining local help, entry fees. Available from the C.P.S.A.
7. 'Western Trap and Skeet Equipment'. Describes the self-loading electric traps. Available from Winchester-Western Division, Olin Mathieson Chemical Corporation, East Alton, Illinois, U.S.A., or Winchester U.K., Site 7, Cutnall Green, Droitwich, Worcs. WR9 ONS.

[219]

8. 'Layouts for Clay Target Shooting'. Obtainable from Eley Ammunition Division, IMI (Kynoch) Ltd., Witton, Birmingham.

9. 'Pamphlets on Traps'. Information on using the hand flinger and installing traps. Published by Imperial Metal Industries.

10. 'The Gun Code'. Safety rules and notes on licences, insurance, nitro-proofing and game seasons. Although mainly for the shooter of live birds it should be read by every owner of a gun. Available from the British Field Sports Society, 59 Kennington Road, London S.E.1.

11. 'Safe Gun Handling'. Pictorial examples of safe and unsafe behaviour with a gun. From *Shooting Times and Country Magazine*, 10 Sheet Street, Windsor, Berks.

12. 'Call for a Bird'. Instructional 16 mm. film. May be had on loan from Imperial Metal Industries.

13. 'Memorandum on the Reproof of Shotguns'. Gives reasons why guns need reproofing. Should be read by anyone contemplating buying a second-hand gun. Incidentally, some cogent reasons are demonstrated each year at the Game Fair at the Proof House stand. Available from The Gun Trade Association, 75 Harborne Road, Birmingham 15.

14. 'Notes on the Purchase of Second-hand Shotguns'. Issued by the Guardians of the Birmingham Proof House, Banbury Street, Birmingham 5.

15. 'A Summary of the law relating to the Possession and Use of Firearms and Ammunition'. The possession, by purchase, gift or borrowing, of airguns, rifles and shotguns and their ammunition is controlled by law with regard to young people under the age of 21. This paper gives details. Available from the Gun Trade Association.